The *Pill* on the *Wall*®

Inspired by ENZOLOGY ™

ENZO TRAPANI, M.D.

Neurologist and Artist

Cover photo by Enzo Trapani
Cover and book design by Cindy Casey
Graphics by Felicia Amon and Shea & Elisa Crawford, Hosting NSB
Positive Affirmation graphic designs by Shea & Elisa Crawford, Hosting NSB

Published by
CCE PUBLISHING
Edgewater, Florida
ccepublishing.com

Printed in the United States of America

Hardback ISBN 979-8-9867617-0-1
Paperback ISBN 979-8-9867617-1-8

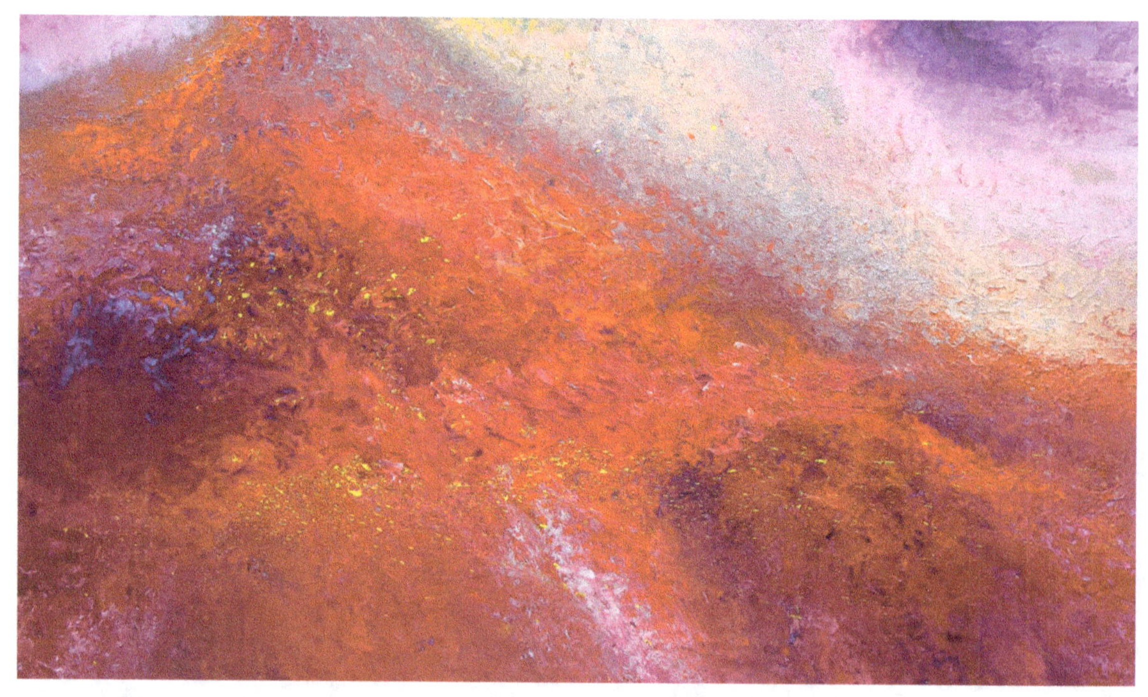

Enzo Trapani art: The Pill on the Wall® series of painting

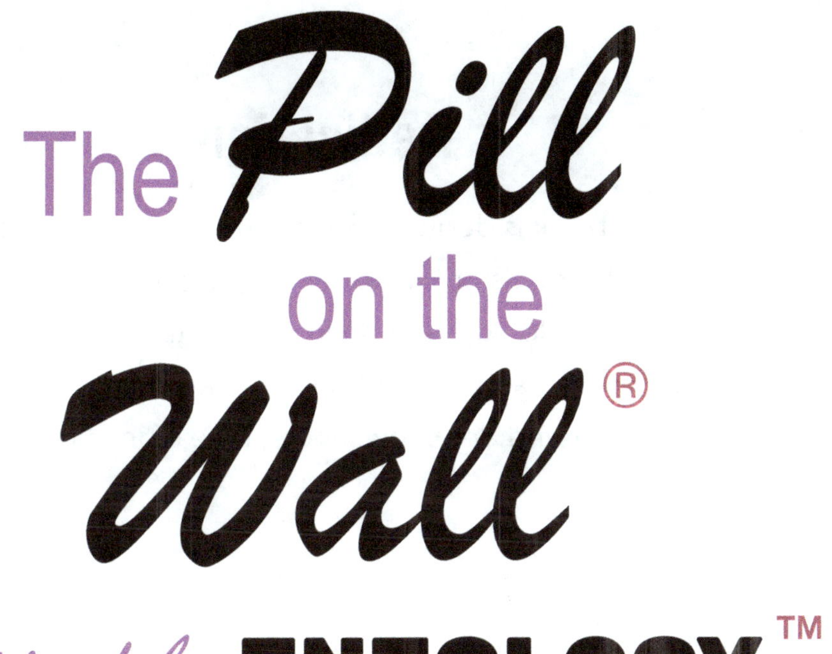

The *Pill* on the *Wall*®

Inspired by **ENZOLOGY**™

Merging science and art for a healthy, long life

ENZO TRAPANI, M.D.

Neurologist and Artist

CCE PUBLISHING
Edgewater, Florida

Dedication

This book is dedicated in memory of my parents;
also to my sister, Lilia, and my daughter, Gabrielle.
This book could not have been done without the dedicated
first-stage editing and great effort of Suzanne Stuckley , M.S., SLP,
forever and deep love and source of inspiration..

Table of Contents

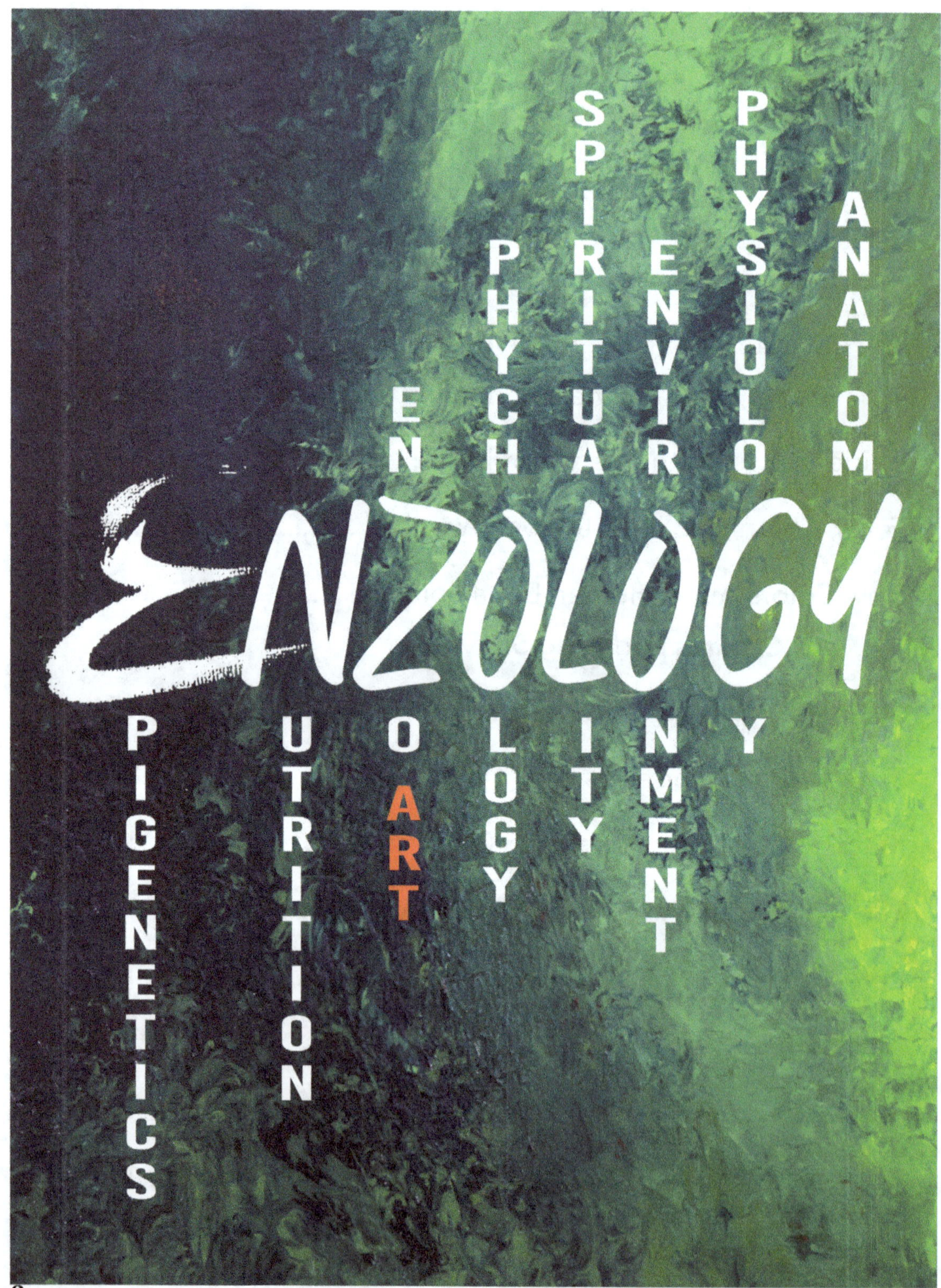

SPIRIT
PHYSIOLOGY
ANATOMY
PHYCHEN
ENVIRONMENT
EPIGENETICS
NUTRITION
ENZOLOGY
ART
OLOGY
CITY

Introduction

Light is life and without the sun we would perish on this planet. We perceive light through colors. As a neurologist and artist, I have come to realize how important colors are in our daily life. In every moment, from birth to waking up every day, the first thing we see is color, which influences us in so many ways.

Color is a vibration of energy. Everyone can see this vibration of energy in different ways, which gives color different meanings.

Knowing how important colors are in our life, I created a field combining art and science, which I call Neuroart.

I first wrote about Neuroart in my medical book titled, Atlas of Electromyography, which was written during my residency in neurology. It was the first time I combined photography with my drawings, explaining how the nervous system works. This book was a great success in the medical field.

Then, using the combination of epigenetics, spirituality, psychology, anatomy, medical illness, neurology, quantum mechanics, physics, environment, physiology and nutrition, I developed two concepts   ENZOLOGY™ and The Pill on the Wall®.

ENZOLOGY™ is a concept that allows one to understand how important and crucial the environment is for everyone. The Pill on the Wall® will give you the color you are lacking. If we are missing a color in us, we have a tendency to love that specific color.

The pill is my art, the wall is your environment.

Because our home is our main environment, we should be aware of the colors that surround us.

It is very important to understand that the environment will change the chemistry in our body, because it changes the expression of the DNA (which is the body protein factory).

I don't intend to change the chemical in our body with my art, I intend to make you aware of the importance of the environment with my art.

There is a relatively new field, which is called Epigenetics. It explains how the environment can change the expression of our own DNA. To understand this concept, I will explain the basis of human cell physiology.

EPIGENETICS
PILL on the Wall
POSITIVE ENVIRONMENT
("COLORS", THOUGHTS, EMOTIONS, PLACES)

CELL-DNA

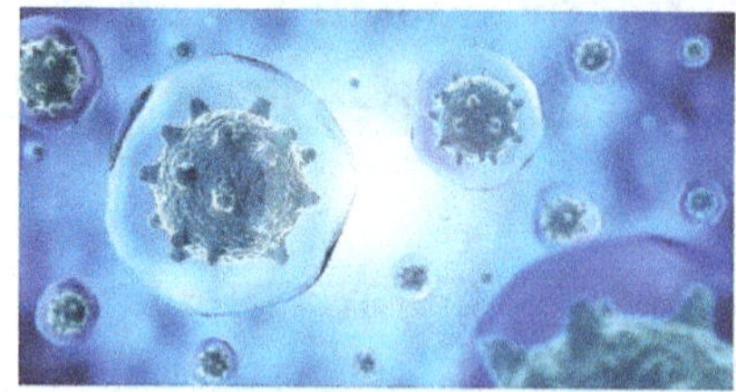

PRODUCE "GOOD" PROTEINS

HEALTHY MIND-BODY

The human body has about 100 trillion cells. Cells are the basic building blocks that contain DNA, or deoxyribonucleic acid. DNA is a molecule in the shape of a double helix, located inside the cell's nucleus.

Inside all DNA, there are more than 20,000 genes. These genes are the protein factory of our body and carry our genetic material information from our family trail (colors of the eyes or hair). It is the environment that changes the expression of the DNA, making us healthier or sicker.

Environment could turn the genes on (becoming active) or off (becoming dormant). The environment consists of everything around us, including what we eat, how we exercise, how we live or interact with people, places where we work and live, and especially our emotional state, including our thoughts.

This explains why stress (environment) or any external unpleasant experience can make us feel ill. The body will release toxic chemicals into the blood stream that can, in the long run, make you feel sick or even develop cancer.

What I am interested in is how colors affect us in our everyday lives, because we see light through colors that are all around us.

During my residency in neurology, I began to notice a pattern at several nursing homes while visiting patients with Alzheimer's disease. I discovered almost all had poor lighting, lack of color and visual cueing, which is essential for orientation and living in general. These homes exhibited a poor environment for their residents and did not promote a positive energy, which would assist in improving memory and general quality of life.

My final thesis, How to Improve the Environment in Nursing Homes and the Impact of their Behavior in Patients with Dementia, was focused on ways to change these living conditions.

This idea stayed dormant for more than 10 years, and later, I started writing this book when I realized I have to place my theory into practice.

I did two projects, the first one was the creation of a house that I called

"Enzology Home," where I painted the house's walls with the right colors and painting for specific areas – green or yellow paintings in the kitchen or living room, light blue painting for the bedroom, orange or red painting for a desk or library area, purple or violet painting for a meditation room.

Also, furniture was rearranged in the right place of the house with the right lighting. Later, I invited friends and family to the Enzology house for feedback. I received a positive response from the majority of my friends.

My second test was the creation of a restaurant, decorated with the same principle, placing my paintings – the Pill on the Wall® – and painting the wall with the same concept. The result was that people began to stay longer in this more appealing environment, which promoted more socialization.

I even created a formula that explains that love is light and how important it is to be in a positive environment, because being in a positive environment will create joy and good health.

We perceive light through colors and we all need love to make it pos-

Enzology formula

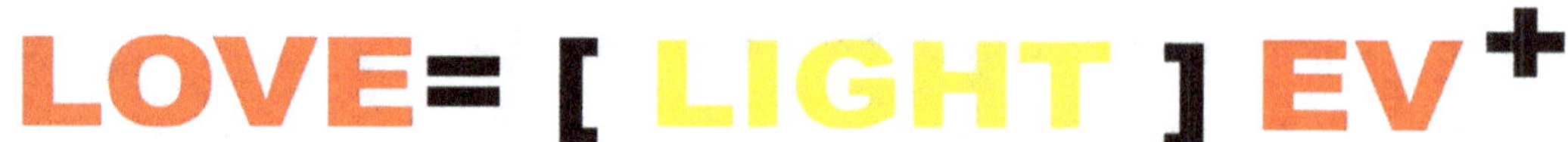

sible. I mention love because I define love as the creating force of the universe, like gravity or a magnetic field with a powerful attraction force. We all need some degree of love to be attracted to any material or emotional subject, knowing that all external reality has colors.

I believe LOVE has no opposition because it is a natural force and is the natural state of being. Evilness or darkness is our own creation.

Believe

The ability to BELIEVE is imperative. The moment we start believing, our body chemically changes for better or for worse, depending on the content of our thoughts. This explains why the placebo effect is so powerful.

From the moment we believe, changes in the universe occur since thoughts are vibrations of energy, comparable to a big antenna sending a constant signal in and out of ourselves.

The most important concept of ENZOLOGY™ is to realize how color influences us in our everyday lives: how we are able to get to know ourselves better through colors and the crucial importance of the environment.

In this book, I will explain the history of colors from the beginning of art thousands of years ago to the current art movement. In different chapters, I will describe how we perceive colors (the anatomy and physiology), the physicist aspect, spirituality, quantum mechanics (study of the subatomic level of things), the importance of nutrition, causes of physical illness, and the psychology of colors. Included throughout the book are positive affirmations, or motivational lines of inspiration and knowledge.

Nutrition

Nutrition is the key, but it is not everything.

When it comes to nutrition, many things can be said. You can never be wrong eating natural foods, including fruit and vegetables, and you can never overdo. I believe eating meat in moderation cannot be detrimental for your health.

I have to mention a very comprehensive study done in recent years. It was called "The China Study" (the bible of vegans), which took more than 20 years and was conducted by Dr. T. Colin Campbell, PhD.

The study included more than 6,000 people from 65 rural counties in China and examined the link between the consumption of animal products (including dairy) and diabetes, cancer and coronary artery disease.

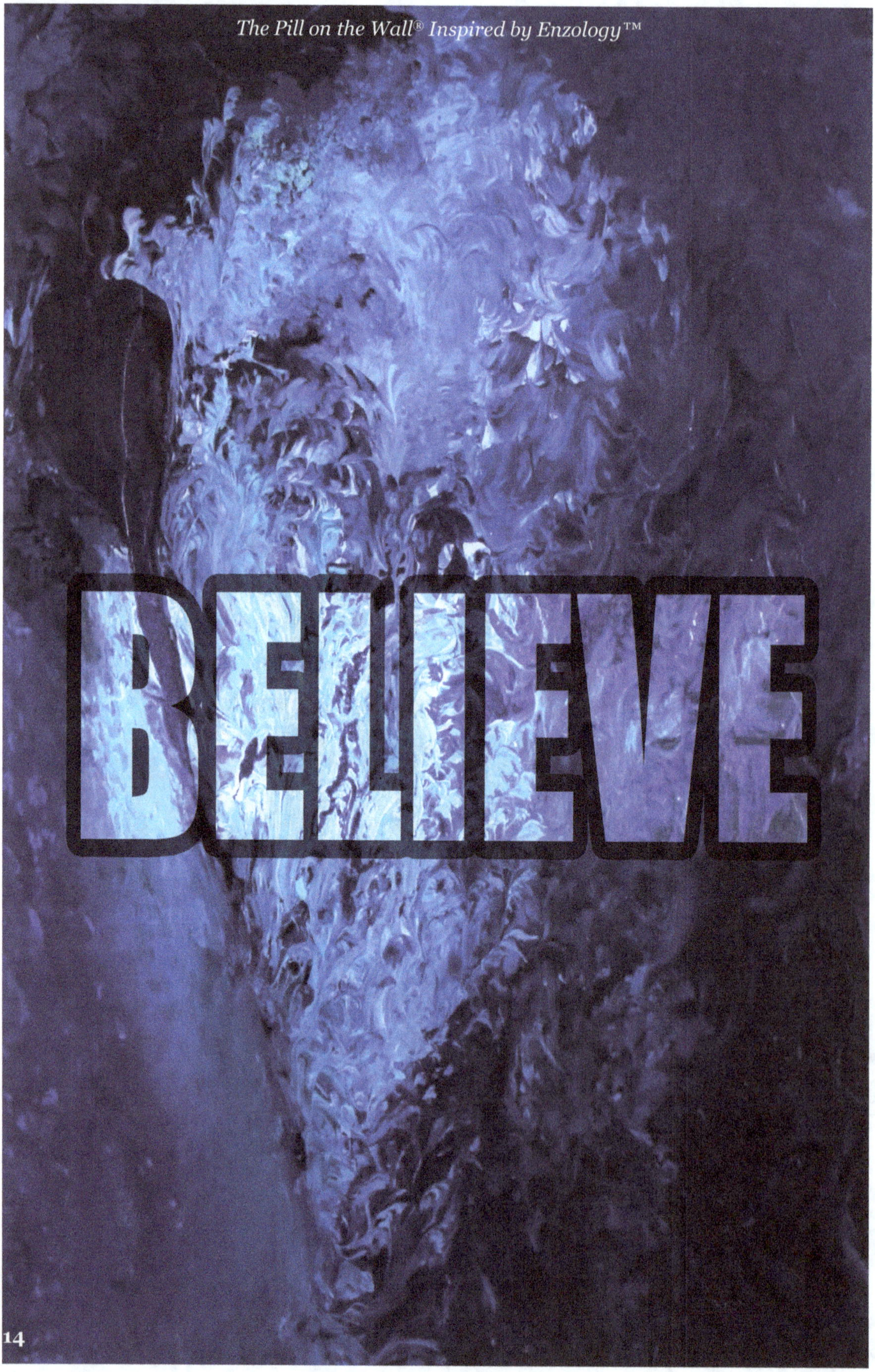

The Pill on the Wall® Inspired by Enzology™

The study was clear, showing concrete evidence that eating animal-based protein is more likely to cause cancer and heart disease than plant-based protein, and advocates eating protein from nuts, lentils, soy, beans, or broccoli.

Even if you have all the possible knowledge on nutrition and health, I personally believe that moderation is the key when it comes to nutrition.

It is not always about the type of food we eat, but the way we eat it. For example: eating an organic carrot and watching toxic local news on TV by yourself is more detrimental that eating homemade spaghetti with meatballs on a long table surrounded by friends and family, laughing and spending hours with them. The digestion is better because we are adding a positive environment to our meal.

In a later chapter, I will discuss the importance of the soil to get the proper nutrition.

Vision changes as we age

I describe how our vision changes as we age and how different medical illnesses change our perception of interpretation of colors. As we age, our vision declines in performance, our pupils become smaller and the eyes can become cloudy, causing them to need three times more light to see.

Dementia and stroke are two of the most common illnesses I encounter in my daily practice of neurology. Both can cause abnormalities of the visual pathway and perception of colors. Lack of sunlight in some countries can cause depression, known as seasonal affective disorder. The treatment for this type of depression is light therapy.

As we know, the sun radiates light. Light is made of three things: wavelength (the distance between two crests of waves), frequencies (the number of crests passing a particular point per second, cycles per second is called Hertz), and energy (photons). Color is the only visible light from the sun that we can see.

The sun has high energy radiation, such as ultraviolet, x-ray, and gamma

The Light

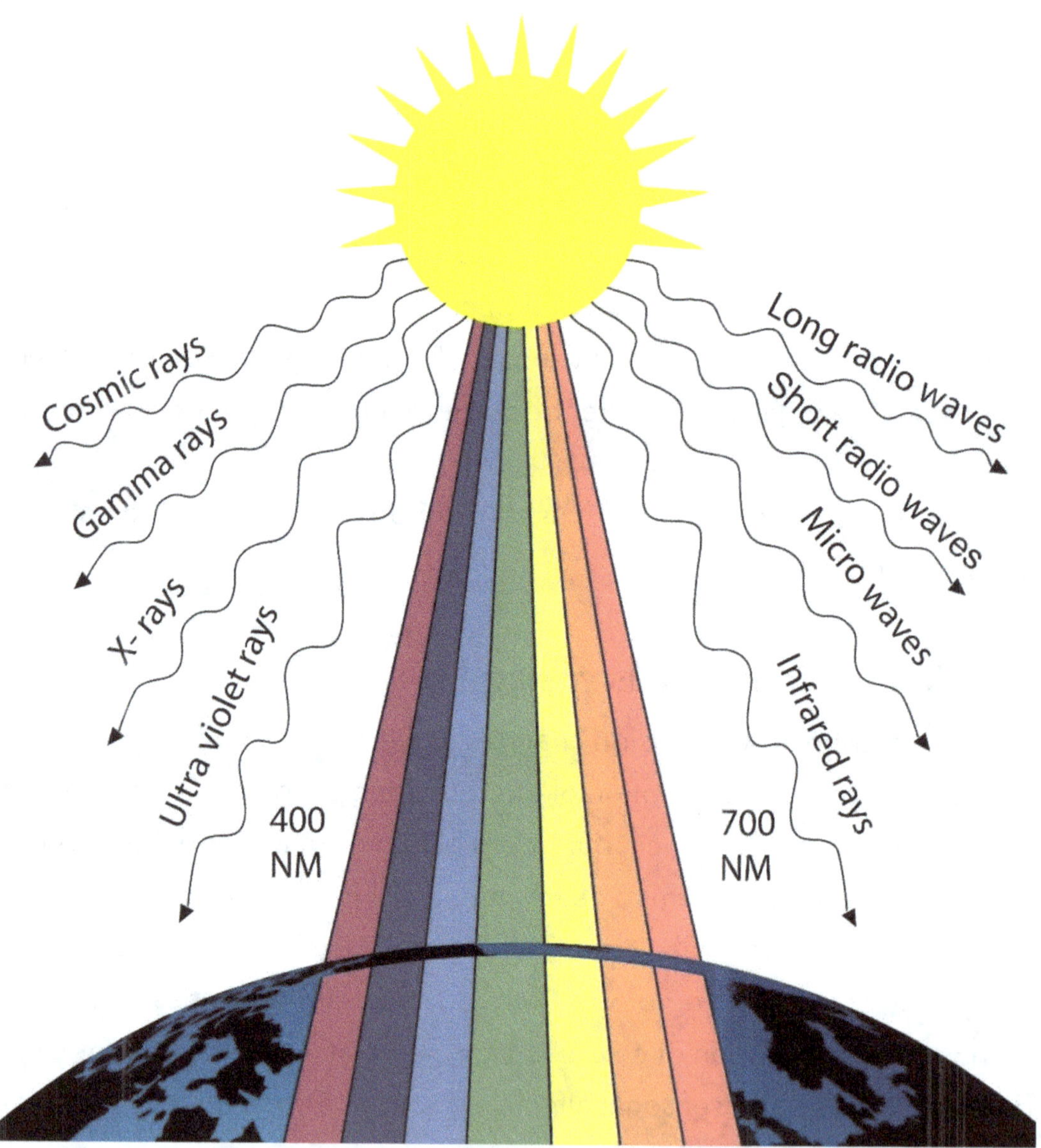

rays, which are dangerous to our health. Light also has low energy radiation consisting of radio waves, microwaves, infrared, and visible light (colors).

Many of us learned the basis of color in our early school years. We learned that primary colors are red, blue and yellow, and with these three colors, we can make any color.

RED has the longest wavelength and decreased frequency (low energy)

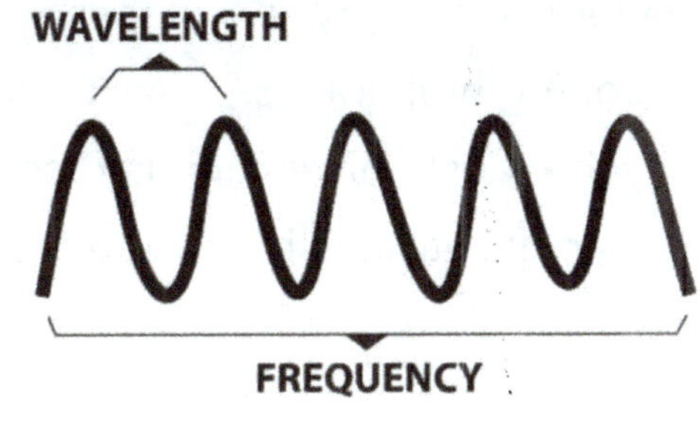

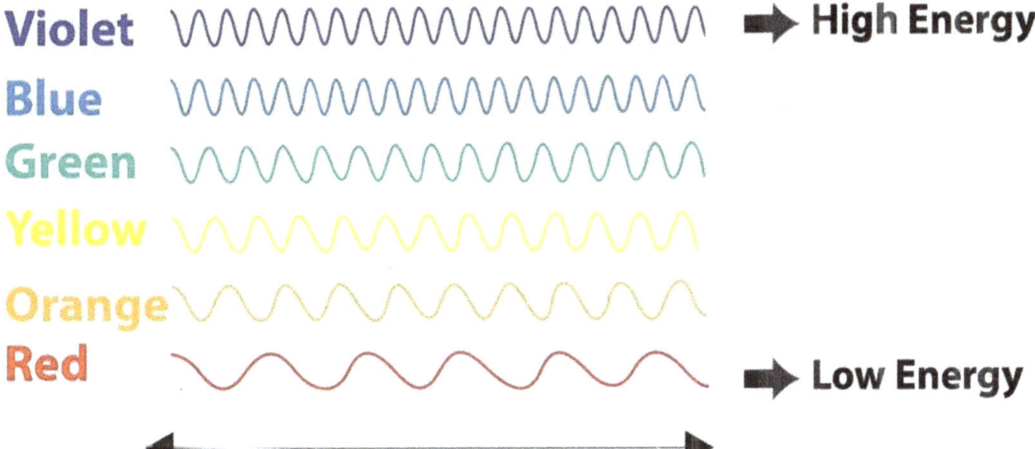

on the spectrum of colors. It is known as a warm color. Red brings warmth, stimulation, and symbolizes high energy. This color carries a lot of meanings: vitality, courage, passion, sexuality, love, joy, anger, socialism or communism (East Europe or China), self-confidence, and exciting emotions.

Even our blood is red because we carry an iron-based protein called hemoglobin, which becomes red when combined with oxygen, and is then transported all throughout the body by red blood cells. Red is in our own bloodstream.

On the chakra chart, red is located at the base of the spine and represents survival, self-confidence and being grounded.

Chakras are the center of energy in our body, which include psychological, emotional, mental and non-physical states.

BLUE is another primary color and falls in the high frequency (high energy) and shorter wavelength of the visible light spectrum. It is known as a cool color. Blue usually represents being calm and relaxation. It is associated with peace, trust, integrity, and loyalty. Blue may reduce stress and slow down the metabolism, inspiring high ideals. It has been said that it is the color of the spirit. It is probably the most universally liked color. However, in the food industry, blue may be unappetizing since there are not many natural foods with this color. Having dinner plates with this color may suppress the appetite.

On the Chakra chart, blue sits on the base of the throat and represents self-expression, trust and communication.

YELLOW is another primary color in the middle of the visible light spectrum and is known as a warm color. It is the brightest color in the spectrum, which is the reason it is used for pedestrian street crossings. It represents creativity, happiness, optimism, and enthusiasm. The color yellow helps us to focus better, recall information, and is the color of communication and networking. It helps us with decision making and to clarify our thoughts, but yellow in excess can also produce anxiety or agitation.

On the chakra chart, yellow is located in the solar plexus. It represents

Chakras

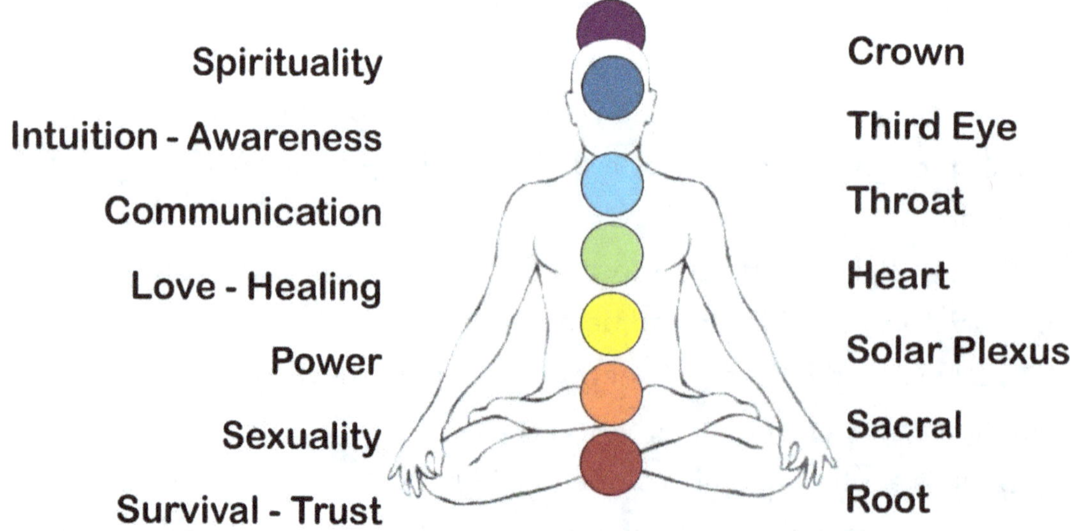

OUR MIND AND HEART ARE FREQUENTLY INTERCEPTED BY CULTURAL NORMS

self-esteem, personal power and will.

The Color Wheel

Like everything else in life, when we have proper knowledge, we have harmony. When we have ignorance, we end up with chaos. There is no doubt that in a positive environment, we are healthier.

Being surrounded by the right colors allows us to get to know ourselves better.

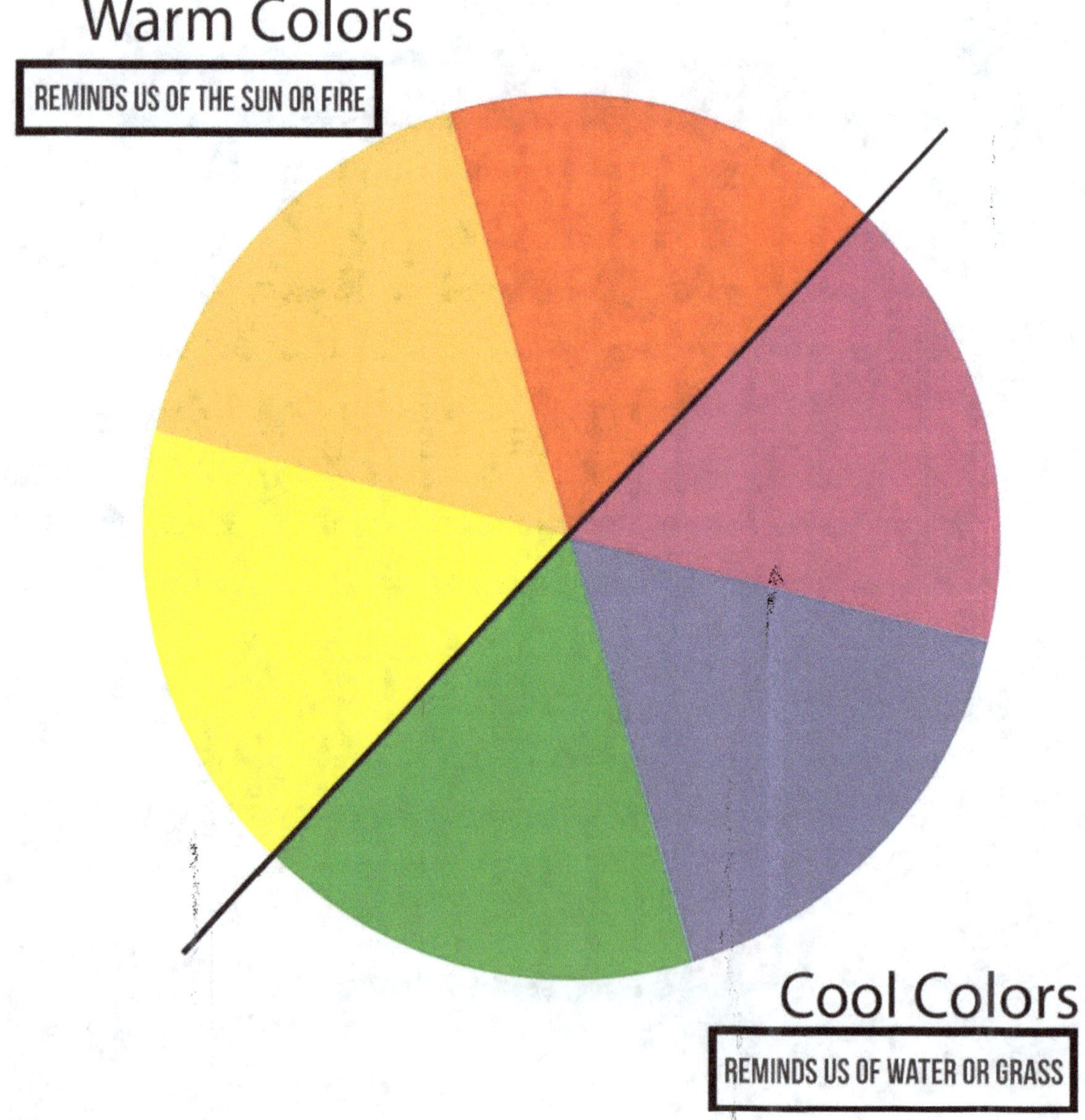

Remember that when we love a specific color, it means that we are lacking that specific color represented in us and we need more of it. It is comparable to lacking specific nutrients in our meals or emotions in our lives.

Our main essence is not about dividing ourselves by race, age, ethnicity, politics, language, gender or religion, but to unify ourselves with love through colors.

To clarify the ENZOLOGY™ concept, behind each of my paintings there are two main meanings:

- Awareness of the environment (through epigenetics) which helps you to realize the importance of it, because it will change the expression of your genetic material in the DNA (positive thoughts create positive proteins in your body, negative thoughts create the opposite).
- You love the color that is missing in you (PILL ON THE WALL®).

The pill is my art, the wall is your environment.

It is my intention to share my knowledge on how colors impact your health and well-being.

INTUITION IS OUR MASTERPIECE

The History of Art and Color

One of the most fascinating stories is how colors evolved through history. It is said that one of the first pigments was invented about 40,000 years ago by combining charcoal and burning animal fat with soil.

Since that time, different movements were created from the time of the Stone Age to Contemporary art. Because of the evolution of art, I realized why we love and appreciate today's art.

Prehistoric Art (40,000-4,000 BC)

During the prehistoric era, life was not easy and the main goal was to hunt in order to survive. Art was concentrated in caves and this period was marked by the rise of homo sapiens and the ability to create tools and weapons.

During the Mesolithic era (10,000-8,000 BC), life became a little easier for homo sapiens because ice began to retreat. The art moved out of caves and on to rock, which allowed for engraving small sculptures. The most extensive collection of Mesolithic rock art has been found on the Mediterranean coast of Spain.

Most of the art was created by using natural pigments and carving stone to create representations of objects, animals and rituals. The earliest art of this era was found in the caves of Lascaux in France, discovered in 1940.

Ancient Art (4,000 BC-AD 400)

Ancient art was mainly produced by more advanced civilizations with established written languages. These civilizations were from Egypt, Mesopotamia, Greece and Rome.

Several civilizations arose during the Mesopotamia period (3,000-300 BC) like the Sumerian who created temples and sculptures of gods. Stele is a vertical slab of stone often inscribed with text or some type of relief carving. The Akkadians empire introduced the victory stele, bearing inscriptions and designs.

Later, the Babylonians became a major military power followed by the Assyrians who created elaborate stone carvings, usually showing images of the major events of war.

At last, the Persian empire spanned from Egypt in the west to Turkey in the north throughout Mesopotamia (region of Iran). It was the largest empire the world had ever seen. This Persian empire placed the art on the map (architecture, painting, pottery, calligraphy, metalworking, weaving and pottery).

The Geometric age (1,000-300 BC), whose name is derived from the dominance of geometric forms of the arts, started in Greece and introduced humanistic education for the Ancient Greeks.

Art and technology were closely entwined, and were probably influenced by Plato and Aristotle. These two philosophers resided in Athens. Plato was more abstract and utopian, whereas Aristotle was more empirical, practical and commonsensical.

Art in ancient Egypt was art for the dead. The Egyptians built tombs, pyramids (elaborate tombs), and the Sphinx (also a tomb) and decorated them with colorful pictures of the gods they believed ruled in the afterlife.

Roman art (500 BC) spanned almost 1,000 years and had strong influences from the Greek, Etruscan and the Egyptians. They used broad spectrum materials including marble, painting, silver, bronze, terracotta and mosaic.

The subject of Roman art varies since it was made for private homes of the wealthy or to display in public places. The subject matter ranged from mythological and historical scenes to still lifes and landscapes.

Medieval Art (500-1400)

The Middle Ages, also called The Dark Ages, followed after the fall of the Roman Empire (476 A-C) The Roman Empire was the most powerful economic, political and cultural force in the world. In the early years, the darkness of this art was characterized by brutality and grotesque images. Later, the art was centered on the church, using art to decorate churches with biblical subjects and scenes from classical mythology. One example from this period is the gothic architecture of the Notre Dame church.

Early Christian art is a fascinating topic to me. Religion was a modest and persecuted sect back then and the art was different with a tendency to be more symbolic (a "fish" could allude to Christ, bread and wine invoked the Eucharist).

Crucifixion was most frequently used to punish slaves, pirates or political agitators without civil rights. Later, the cross became the symbol of Jesus Christ.

Constantine the Great (the period of recognition) decreed official toleration of Christianity and subsequently churches and shrines (holy sites dedicated to heroes, saints or martyrs) became filled with large scale relief sculptures and ivory carvings. Walls of churches were decorated with paintings or mosaics.

Byzantine art (526-1400) was born from the Christian Greek artistic products of the Eastern Roman (Byzantine) Empire. It diverged from the early Christian art, and was characterized by being more abstract and symbolic. In the late Byzantine era, Christianity was divided into two distinct camps, the eastern (Orthodox) Christianity and the western (Latin) Christianity.

Renaissance Art (1400-1600)

The characteristics of this art movement were individualism, realism, attention and precision to details on human anatomy. The leading contributors were Leonardo da Vinci, Michelangelo and Raphael.

The Renaissance reached its height in Florence, Italy and probably in large part due to the Medici family. The wealthy family, consisting of bankers and benevolent dictators, sponsored and supported the arts.

This was the Golden Age of Florence and when being an artist became acceptable.

I believe it is important to mention the most important paintings during renaissance paintings:

• **Mona Lisa**, considered to be the single most famous painting, was created by Da Vinci (now displayed at the Louvre Museum in Paris, France).

• **The Last Supper**, a religious scene with Jesus and his twelve apostles, a painting also by Da Vinci, is a fresco located in a church (Santa Maria delle Grazie) found in Milan, Italy.

• **The Creation of Adam** was a painting by Michelangelo, early 1500s, forming the central image on the ceiling of the Sistine Chapels in Rome.

• **The Primavera**, painted by Sandro Botticelli, represents the change of the seasons.

• **The School of Athens** is a fresco painted by Raphael in the early 1500s, featuring almost all the important Greek philosophers of that era.

• **The Birth of Venus**, painted by Botticelli represents the Roman Venus as she arrives on shore having been born at sea and she is delivered on a giant shell.

• **The Sistine Madonna**, painted by Raphael before he died, was the Virgin Mary holding the baby Jesus.

• **The Last Judgment** is a massive fresco painted by Michelangelo on the ceiling of the Sistine Chapel in the Vatican City. He spent four years in the process and originally all the male and female figures were painted nudes, but later were covered up by adding draperies.

• **The Assumption of the Virgin**, painted by Titan in the early 1500s, located at the Basilica in Venice.

• **The Kiss of Judas** (known as the Betrayal of Christ), painted by Giotto di Bondone.

At the end of the Renaissance era, another movement rose and was called Mannerism, characterized by elegance art and sensuous distortion of the human figure. The techniques and skills showed great composition elements, which created a sense of sophisticated elegance. Figures had graceful, elongated limbs and exaggerated details. They were typically influenced by Raphael or Michelangelo, their predecessors.

Baroque Art (1600-1750)

This period of art was characterized by richness and grandeur, with lots of drama and emotions, and used intense contrast of light and dark. The most important artists from this period were the Italian painter Caravaggio and the Dutch painter Rembrandt.

Rococo Art (1700-1750)

Rococo art existed for a brief period. It originated in Paris with significant decorative art, paintings and sculptures. It was characterized by elegance, using natural form and asymmetrical design with subtle colors. Ornaments and theatrical architecture were predominant. Furniture featured curving forms with lots of floral designs.

French painters like Fragonard, Boucher and Watteau were well known in this period.

Neoclassicism (1750-1850)

After ancient civilizations in Athens and Naples were discovered, artists strove to recreate from these classical antiquities, and focus on idealism with harmony and simplicity.

Romanticism (1780-1850)

Romanticism embodied a large range of disciplines from music and literature to painting. It was an intellectual movement that emphasized individualism and emotion. It emphasized greatly into the imagination and embracing the outside with more appreciation of nature. The most prominent artists include Thomas Cole, Blake and Constable.

Realism (1848-1900)

Realism began in France and was the result of an anti-Romantic movement in Germany and the rise of photography and journalism. Artists were committed to paint only what they could see, embracing more light and colors. Well known artists include Gustave Courbet and Jean Francois Millet (with his work: The Angelus).

Impressionism (1865-1885)

The artists captured a particular moment (impression), such as a painting of a sailboat regatta or a dancer instead of concentrating on mythological history. The work was short with quick and unfinished brushstrokes.

The most prominent artist of impressionism was Claude Monet, a French artist, whose works include The Water Lily Pond and Impression Sunrise.

Post-impressionism (1885-1910)

The painters concentrated on personal meaning with a subjective vision and a touch of abstract lines. They were a group of artists who moved past Impressionism, including the great Vincent van Gogh, Seurat, Gauguin and Cezanne. This art evoked more emotion than realism, and consisted of symbolic motifs and lots of brushstrokes.

Fauvism (1900-1935)

Fauvism was led by Henry Matisse. This 20th century movement showed intense color, line and brushwork with flat composition using brilliant colors applied straight from the paint tube. It created a sense of explosion.

Expressionism (1905-1920)

Expressionism was an art movement in which the image of reality was distorted by the feeling and raw emotions of the artist. Art became expressive and possibly emerged as a response to the increasing world conflict.

One of the most prominent expressionist artists was Edvard Munch with the famous work, The Scream.

Cubism (1907-1914)

Cubism started with Pablo Picasso and Gorges Braque. Art forms were broken down into geometric shape forms of cubes, inspiring the first abstract concept. In essence, these artists rejected the concept that art should be a copy of nature.

Surrealism (1915-1950)

Surrealism was about expressing the subconscious and hidden meaning of dreams. It was at that time that Sigmund Freud (Austrian neurologist, 1856-1939) became the founder of the psychoanalytic school of psychology, influencing artists like Salvador Dali.

This movement emerged from the birth of the Dada movement, which was from the reaction of capitalism, nationalism and corrupt politics. Dada was a reactionary art and a philosophical movement to protest against what they saw in World War I. One of the most ubiquitous artists of this movement was Marcel Duchamp and his most iconic art piece was titled Fountain (1917).

Abstract Expressionism (1940s-1950s)

Abstract expressionism emerged in New York after WWII and it may be referred to as Action Painting. It incorporated lots of improvisation, raw emotion and spontaneity in large sizes. Celebrating artists were Jackson Pollock and Mark Rothko.

Op and Pop art (1950s-1960s)

Op art, short for Optical art, used shapes, colors and patterns that appeared to be moving, with zigzag black and white lines. One of the most prominent artists was Bridget Riley.

Pop art was the art that used everyday objects and embraced consumerism. The most famous pop art was created by Andy Warhol with his piece Campbell's Soup Cans.

Art Povera (1960s)

Art povera means "poor art" and this movement took place in Italy. Artists used rocks, soil, rope and other elements challenging contemporary systems. Therefore, many of these types of art were sculptures. A well-known artist during this movement was Mario Merz.

Minimalism (1960s-1970s)

This movement started in New York, as a combination of art and design, especially as visual art. It eliminated the non-essential forms and concentrated on purity and giving order, harmony and simplicity to things.

The artist avoided emotional meaning, instead paying attention to the material of the work.

Famous artists were Frank Stella, Robert Morris and the most renounced architect was Frank Lloyd Wright.

Conceptual Art (1960s-1970s)

Conceptual art emerged as an art movement in the mid-60 s, rejecting previous art movements and creating art in a form of performance. It could be almost anything. There was not one style or form and the concept behind the work was more important than the finished art object. It was a radical and controversial movement and some experts dismissed it as art.

The art was created by the viewer, not by the artist or the artwork itself. All art was conceptual.

Some of the current conceptual artists of this time are Jenny Holzer and Marina Abramovic (a Serbian performance artist who brought a relationship between the artist and the audience).

Contemporary Art (1970s-Present)

Contemporary art is responsible for bringing art to the present time and is dominated by various schools and different movements, including Post-Modernism, Feminism, Neo-Expressionism, Street (graffiti) and Digital art.

This art movement has been described as a reaction to modern art (Impressionism), reflecting a society that applauds technology, globalism and cultural diversity. Some art writers say that contemporary art began with Pop art (pioneered by Roy Lichtenstein and Andy Warhol), representing mass culture.

Feminist art was a feminist movement, highlighting the difference women can make to society, breaking gender stereotypes and promoting increased independence of women. Icon artists were Judy Chicago, Georgia O'Keeffe and Frida Kahlo.

One of the art movements that most intrigued me was graffiti art, since it became notoriously prominent in New York City and it is derived from the Italian word graffio. It has a long history since this type of art has been found in the Maya city of Tikal and in ancient Roman ruins.

During the 20th century, the art was associated with gangs and illegal places. It was prominent in major urban centers, created with spray paint on building walls, and was a type of self-expression that I believe started to gain attention since it was in public places functioning outside art galleries.

Two of the most prominent graffiti artists were Revok and Banksy (an anonymous England-based Street artist). Banksy is a political activist, who used satirical street art with dark humor.

The History of Color

RED

Red pigments were one of the first colors used and were found on cave walls in Altamira, Spain (dated between 15000 and 165000 BC). Red, along with white and black, was a color used by artists in the Paleolithic age, since it could be obtained from nature. The red ochre was a common color to paint the body.

Later in the 16th century, an insect from Mexico called Cochineal, a white bug that produced a potent non-toxic red pigment, was used by well re-nowned artists. The Cochineal can be sun-dried, crushed and dipped in an acidic alcohol solution to produce the acid or pigment of red.

BLUE

Blue is another color with a long history. It was synthesized around 2200 B.C. during Ancient Egypt times when the pyramids were built. The ultramarine blue was made from a semiprecious gemstone, Lapis Lazuli, originating in the Afghanistan mountains and was very pricey back in the 6th century.

YELLOW

It is thought that the oldest yellow pigment was the yellow ochre, used by the Egyptians and ancient civilizations. The yellow ochre pigment was found in an image of a horse in the Lascaux cave, a prehistoric cave in southwestern France, estimated to be 17,000 years old.

GREEN

Mixing yellow and blue, green was created, and was used by Egyptians and Greeks. The Greeks introduced verdigris, one of the first artificial pigments. Verdigris was obtained by applying acetic acid to copper plates. In history, green pigments were used in several poisonous substances.

PURPLE

It is not a color that is usually found in nature and was used to dye clothing. Since it was expensive and hard to obtain, purple was the color worn by

Roman emperors to show wealth (1900 B.C).

WHITE

The color white has no hue. The reason the color is white is because it reflects all visible wavelengths of the light spectrum.

This color was often found in old caves. White was used by Romans, Ancient Egyptians and Greeks. The meaning of white varies from mourning to purity, depending on the country it is presented in.

BLACK

The opposite of white, black is also an achromatic (no hue) color. The reason it is black is because of the complete absorption of the visible wavelength light spectrum. It has also been found in old caves and the pigment was created by burning bones. It was back in the time of the Roman Empire that black was associated with mourning.

The Influence of Color

During different centuries and with various cultures, each color represents different meanings.

Colors influence us in every moment of our existence, from our birth and throughout our life experiences.

Cinematography is a clear example. Film production started in the 1890s and motion pictures were created, but due to poor technology, the films did not last more than a few minutes and were without sound. Films were monochrome (black and white). It was not until the 1960s and 1970s that the television broadcasting stations were able to do the transmission in COLOR.

Introducing colors on the screen allowed us to see movies in a different dimension.

I was always interested in how people dressed (the fashion industry) and the use of make up throughout the history of mankind's evolution. It all started from the homo sapiens when they used different pigments on their bodies for different reasons such as rituals or hunting. Body paintings may have been the earliest way color was used to symbolize specific meanings by using pigments from plants and fruits to tattoo and pierce their body. Cosmetics were used by the ancient Egyptians and the Romans for similar purposes: spiritual life and experience, connection to the divine, sense of oneness, purity and consciousness.

At one time in our history, women used to whiten their skin to be more accepted and fashionable, a contrast with today's appeal. Red lipstick is another statement and was worn by the ancient Sumerians (3,500 BC). In ancient Egypt, both men and women rouged their lips as a symbol of sexuality, whereas with ancient Romans it determined social rank and class.

A painter, poet, sculptor, teacher and theoretician I should mention is Joseph Alberts, born in Germany in 1888, and is considered to be one of the most influential visual artists in the twentieth century. In his book, "Interaction of Color" which was published in 1963, he explained his theory of color, illuminating the visual experience of colors and optical illusions.

He is best known for his iconic series of abstract paintings, the "Homage to the Square" series. He understood that one color could evoke different meanings in people and explained the psychology behind each color. He taught at Yale University, explaining the discrepancy between physical fact and psychic effect of colors.

He wrote, "When you really understand that each color is changed by a changed environment, you eventually find that you learned about life as well as about color."

We are always represented by colors, from the clothes we wear (fashion design), make up choices, hair and nail colors, to the choices of food we consume (eating the rainbow).

Through the history of art, it is very clear to me that art is a form of self-expression and a way to communicate with each other and, consequently, always changes with time – from the way we dress to the way we think.

Art is a reflection of the social, cultural and/or political moments we are living and consequently we appreciate it.

SILENCE ALLOWS US TO CONNECT WITHIN

The Anatomy of Color

Everything in this universe is made of matter and matter is made of atoms.

Atoms are made of extremely tiny particles called protons, neutrons, and electrons. Atoms are also formed by very small particles called quarks and neutrinos.

Electrons were discovered in 1897 by J.J. Thompson. The proton was discovered in 1911 by Ernest Rutherford who was the first to realize that matter is mostly "empty space." Then the neutron was discovered in 1932 by James Chadwick.

Protons and neutrons are in the center of the atom making up the nucleus. Electrons orbit around the nucleus and have negative charge. Protons have a positive charge and neutrons have no charge. Since opposite charges attract, protons and electrons attract each other.

The type of atom is determined by the number of protons. Hydrogen has one proton, helium has two protons, but oganesson has the highest atomic number with 118 protons and has the highest atomic mass. All of these elements are listed in the famous "Periodic Table." Of the 118 elements, only 92 occur in nature, the rest were made in the laboratory.

All matter is made of elements and has mass. In all living organisms, the most common elements found are oxygen, nitrogen, hydrogen, and carbon. Molecules are when atoms bond with other atoms (water has 2 hydrogen atoms and one oxygen atom).

Why do we see objects with specific colors?

Objects appear to have color since they are able to selectively absorb and reflect certain wavelengths of visible light.

The sun generates electromagnetic radiation because it has electric and magnetic fields, creating what is called the electromagnetic spectrum. In that spectrum, we only see the visible light or visible spectrum (the rainbow).

THE ATOM

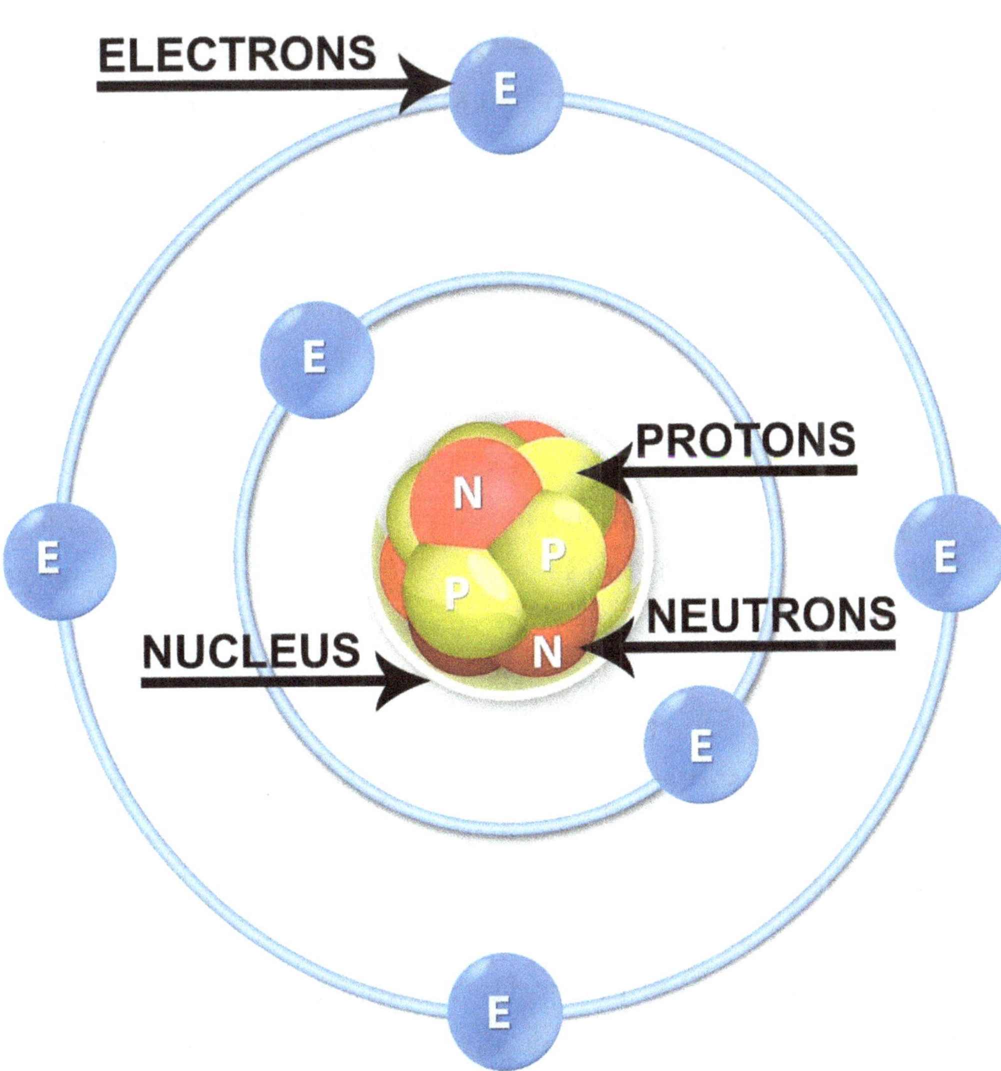

Light has wavelength, frequency and energy.

Wavelength: the distance between peaks of each wave.

Frequency: the number of wave peaks that pass by per second.

Light is made up of wavelengths of light, and each wavelength is a particular color. The color we see is a result of which wavelengths are reflected to the retina in the back of our eyes. This activates the cones and rods, which are the small cells responsible for sending the color signals to the brain.

Color is actually specific energies of light waves which fall into the ranges of visible spectrum between red and violet. We see objects as a specific color because of the color effect. For example, when a red object is hit with light rays from the sun, the object reflects only red light and absorbs all other light.

Objects will appear BLACK when it absorbs all wavelengths of visible light. However, objects will appear WHITE when it does not absorb any wavelength of visible light. This is the reason we wear white colors on a hot and sunny day to reflect the light.

The typical explanation of how important it is to understand how light works is the example of the frozen sea water of the Arctic. As soon as the sunlight hits the icy, frozen water of the Arctic, it will reflect a lot of the sunlight back into the atmosphere since white will not absorb light, keeping cool temperatures in that region. However, if the ice sheets are not there, the ocean water will absorb the rest of the sunlight, increasing the water temperature. Melting ice in the Earth's Poles (the North and South Pole) and glaciers contributes to sea level rise.

In summary, we see any objects with color based on how much wavelengths of light it absorbs or is reflected by the object.

The way we can see light is through "colors." For a long time, it was a debate to determine if light traveled through particles or waves. Photon (the particle of light) behaves like a particle and a wave, simultaneously.

One point of view envisions light as waves, producing energy that

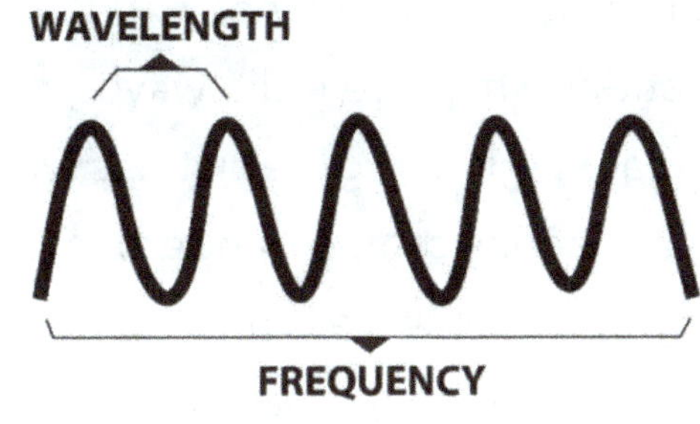

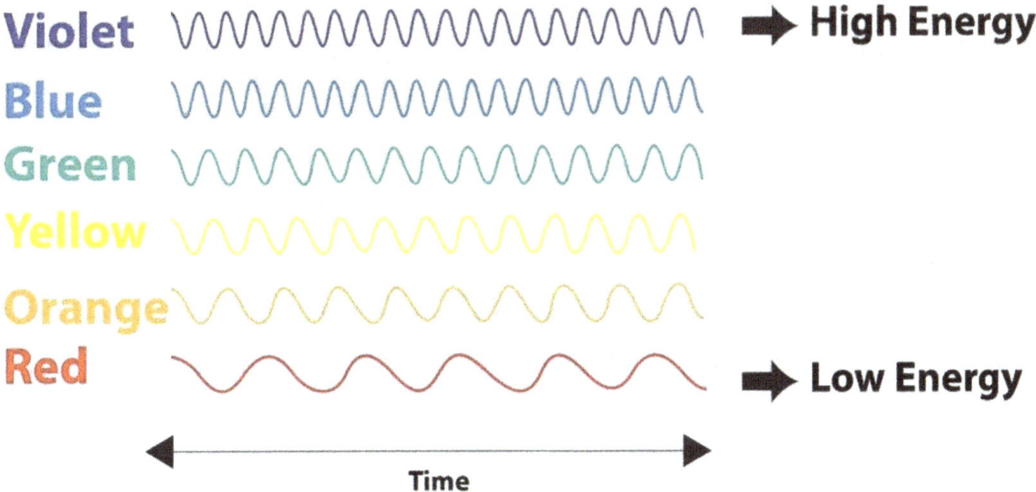

travels through space. Like in nature, it compares in a manner similar to the rip- ples spreading across the surface of a still pond after being disturbed by a dropped rock. The opposing view holds that light is composed of a steady stream of particles (photons), much like tiny droplets of water sprayed from a garden hose nozzle. During the past few centuries, the consensus of opinion has wavered with one view prevailing for a period of time, only to be over- turned by evidence for the other. Only during the first decades of the twentieth century was there enough compelling evidence collected to provide a compre- hensive answer. To everyone's surprise, both theories were correct.

Different colors of light have different wavelengths and different energies. Short wavelengths mean they have more energy and the shorter the wavelength, the higher the frequency. Light speed remains the same.

Short wavelength means higher frequency and more energy (violet).
Longer wavelength means less frequency and less energy (red).

The sun radiates light to our planet with different energy radiation. There are low energy radiations which are radio waves, microwaves, infrared and visible light. Also, there are high energy radiations which are ultraviolet, x-ray and gamma rays. These radiations can be dangerous to our health.

The frequency of a light wave is how many waves move past a certain point during a set amount of time, usually in one second. Frequency is generally measured in hertz. Hertz is a measurable unit and is defined as one cycle per second. Color is the frequency of visible light, and it ranges from 430 trillion hertz (which is red) to 750 trillion hertz (which is violet).

The electromagnetic energy travels as waves that vary based on the wavelength. Radio waves or microwaves have long wavelengths and low frequencies. X Rays and Gamma Rays have short wavelengths and high frequencies. The fusion explosion of the hypernova (explosion of the star) generates gamma rays (high beam frequency) with intense energy so powerful that it can be detected as far as 10 billion light years away from planet earth.

All these light energies travel at the same speed. The light speed is the speed the light wave propagates (186,000 miles/sec or 300,000 km/sec).

To demonstrate how fast light can travel, light can go around the planet earth 7.5 times in one second.

Light moves incredibly fast, but over the vast scale of the universe, the light speed is less noticeable. Because the universe is so vast, we use light-year, which is the distance a beam of light travels in a single Earth year. For example, from your comfortable chair in your house, to reach the edge of the universe, light has to travel 13.8 billion light years.

One light year is 5.8 trillion miles. Knowing this simple fact, I find it difficult that we are alone in this universe.

I believe the universe is in us. If you look inside yourself, you may feel the vast space and the unlimited potential you possess.

One interesting fact is that when we are looking at the sky, we are looking at the light generated from the stars, but the light generated by that specific star we are observing was generated many light years ago. We are

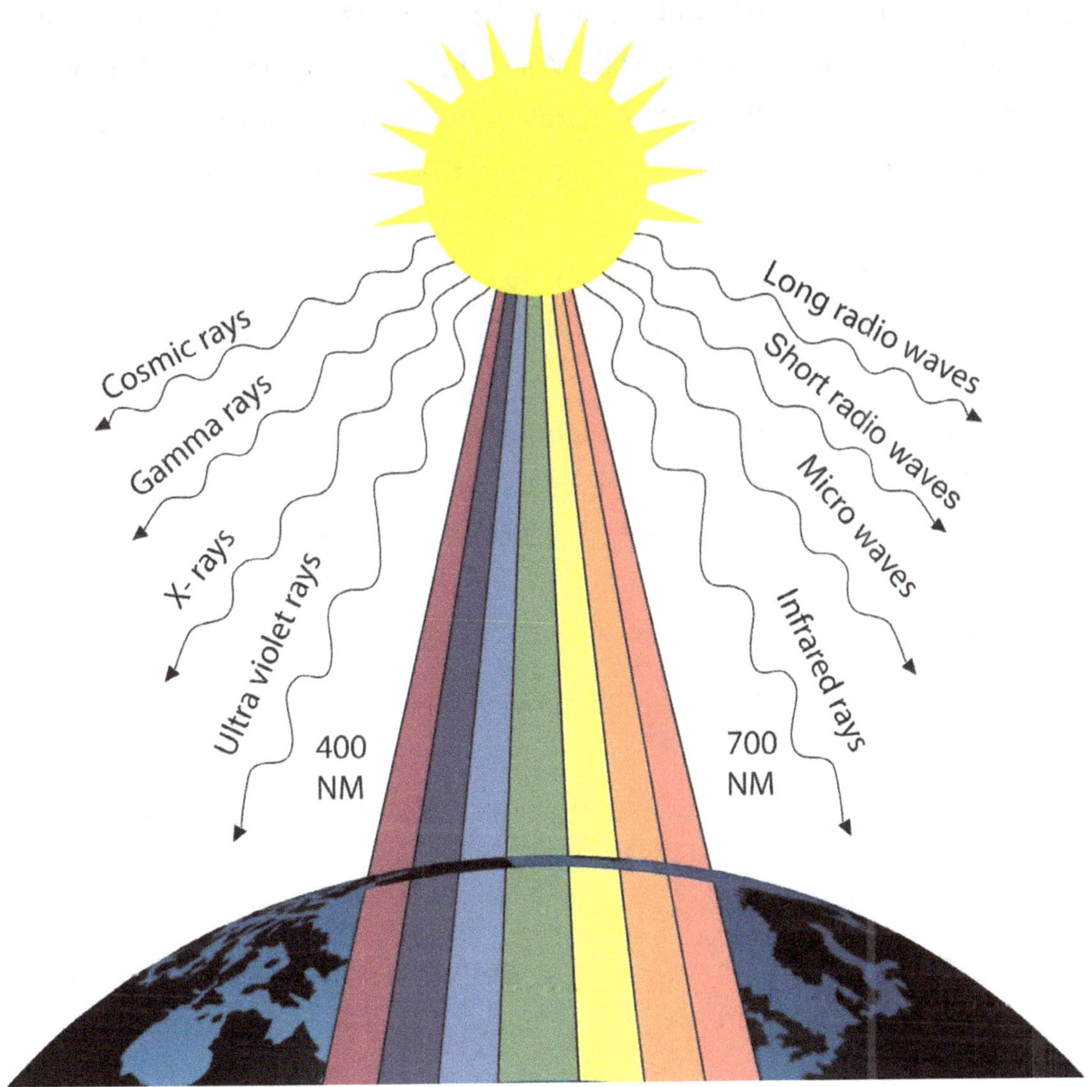

looking into the Milky Way.

It has been established that the universe is 13.8 billon years old.

In ancient Greek and Roman times, it was believed Earth was the center of the universe. This is known as the geocentric model.

In the sixteenth century, Copernicus, Kepler, and Galileo established that the sun goes around the planet Earth. This is known as the heliocentric model, which was helped with the discovery of the telescope in 1608.

For centuries, it was thought that the Milky Way was an entire universe. However, in 1924 an astronomer named Edwin Hubble found a nebula (a cloud of gas in outer space) and stumbled upon Andromeda (our neighboring galaxy). It was later realized that the Milky Way is one of many galaxies. The Andromeda and the Milky Way galaxies are about 2.5 million light-years apart.

Today, the observable universe is estimated to have more than two trillion galaxies.

We are made of the same crucial elements as the stars in the universe which are hydrogen, oxygen, nitrogen, sulfur, carbon and phosphorus.

We carry the universe inside.

Those six components are the elements of life.

It is true to say that human beings are made of stardust. Humans and the universe (galaxies) have about 97 percent of the same atoms.

The Color Wheel

Let's look at the color wheel. I'll show you how colors relate to and complement each other.

Red, yellow and orange are warm colors. Blue, green and violet are cool colors. If you look at the color wheel, the warm colors are on one side of the wheel and the cools on the other.

Warm colors produce more energy from the cultural and psychological point of view. Cool colors are calmer.

RED, YELLOW AND BLUE ARE PRIMARY COLORS. Primary colors cannot be made from other colors. Artists create all the other colors of the rainbow by mixing together the primary colors.

GREEN, ORANGE AND VIOLET ARE SECONDARY COLORS. Secondary colors are made by mixing two primary colors. Each secondary color is made from the two primary colors closest to it on the color wheel.

Tertiary colors are formed by mixing a primary and a secondary color together. There are six tertiary colors; red-orange, yellow-orange, yellow-green, blue-green, blue-violet, and red-violet. Tertiary colors help to create a nice rainbow.

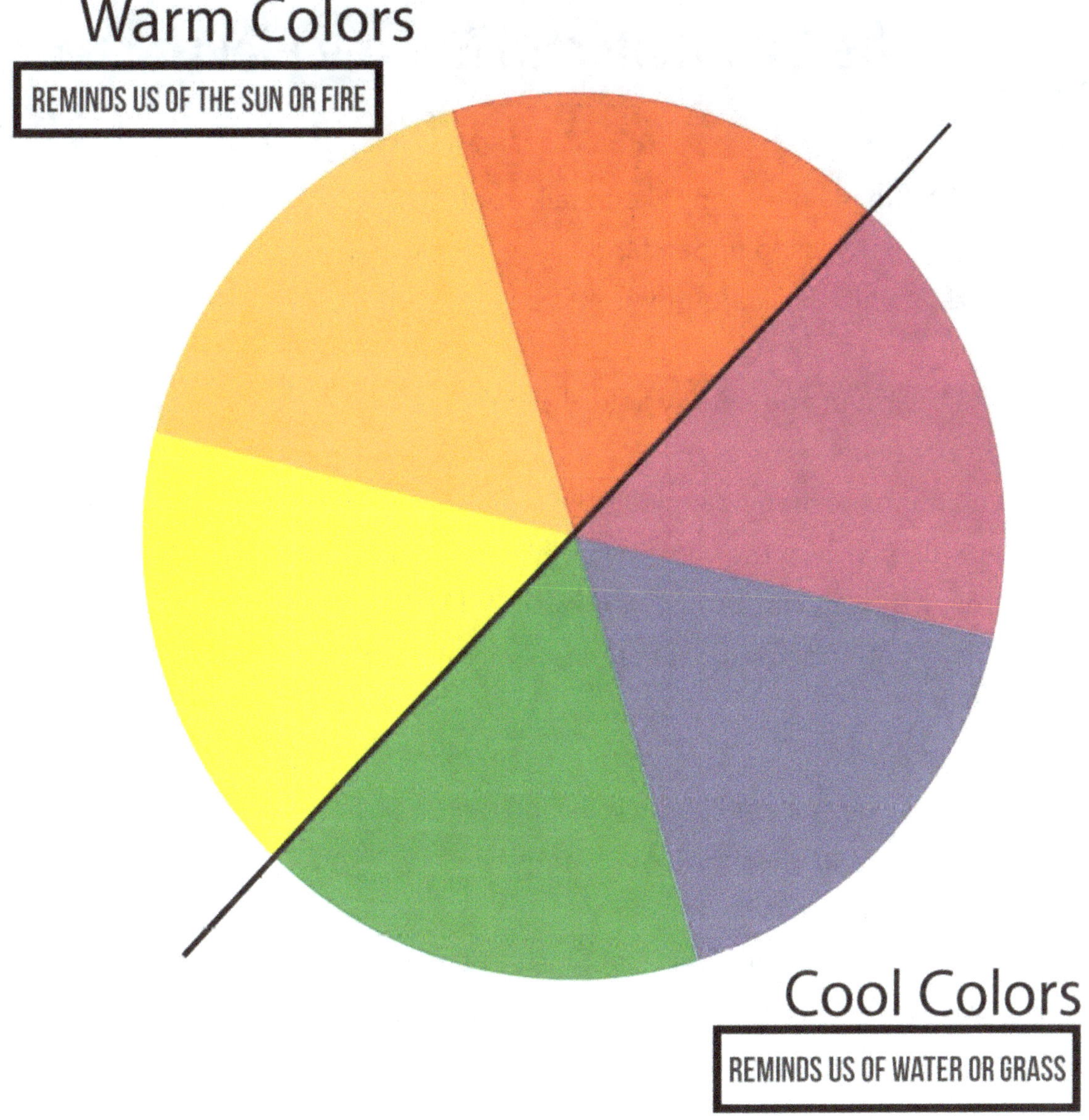

Our most important energy source is light and the spectrum of colors is derived from light. Sunlight, which contains all the wavelengths, consists of the entire electromagnetic spectrum that we depend on to exist on this planet.

The Quantum and Energy Field

The main reason I like to talk about the quantum field is because it helps us to understand all we see, feel and touch is energy, which is all around us. It is our environment and we see it as matter.

The quantum and energy fields hold the keys of happiness, joy, love and faith for a better life.

Quantum mechanics explains the composition of matter and how matter interacts with energy at the very subatomic level. The concept and theory of Quantum mechanics was born in the early 1900s. Quantum physics can partially explain matter behavior at the most intimate level and unfold the definition of reality.

Albert Einstein was a German-born physicist who created the Theory of Relativity. While he was one of the most influential physicists in the modern time, he could not explain how the quantum field worked since it doesn't follow the rules of the physical world.

I admire the beautiful mind of Einstein because he was able to explain how gravity worked (in the fabric of space-time). He accomplished these three hundred years after the mathematician and physicist Isaac Newton attempted to explain in his book, "Principia," the law of motion and gravity. However, I do not think Newton completely understood how gravity worked.

It is said that if you understand how quantum mechanics work, it is because you do not understand it. That is how complicated it can be.

Reality is all that we see and we see in color, which is a vibration of energy made of photons (the particle of light).

Daily, we become impregnated by a field of information of colors affecting our body and thoughts. When the colors reach our mind, we can respond in a positive or negative way, depending on the meaning we give to that spe-

QUANTUM FIELD

REALITY: "THE COLLAPSE OF THE WAVE-FUNCTION BY THE OBSERVER"

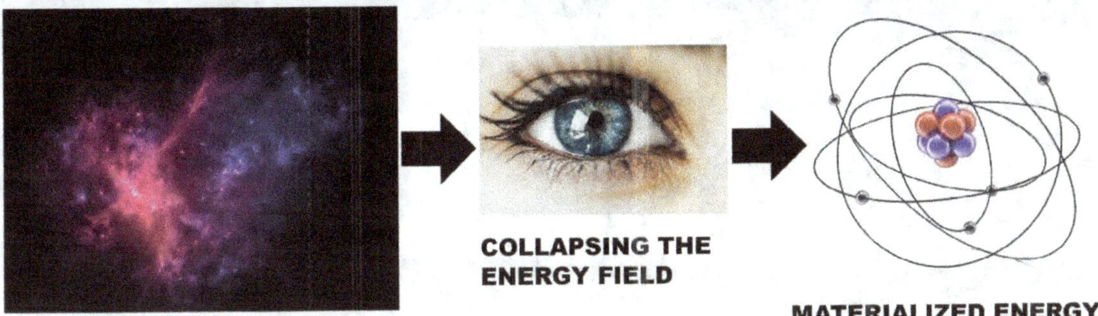

SUB-ATOMICAL PARTICLES: PROTONS, NEUTRONS ELECTRONS, NEUTRINOS, (Quarks)

cific color.

Now, let's breakdown quantum.

By definition, "quantum reality is the collapse of wave function by the observer." To understand this definition, I will explain some universal laws.

There was an interesting experiment called "The Double Slit" or "Young's Experiment." It explained how matter can behave like particles (electrons) or waves depending on the observer. A clear explanation is demonstrated in the animated YouTube video, "Dr. Quantum, Double Slit Experiment." It is a clip from the movie "What the Bleep Do We Know!?"

It demonstrates how the mind shapes how we perceive things in the universe. In a simple explanation, when electrons pass through the slit without being observed, the electrons behave like waves. However, when the electrons pass through the slit and are being observed, they act like matter. It appears the electrons behave differently when being observed. Remember that electrons are tiny particles of matter.

When the observer is not seeing or paying attention to the   matter, these electrodes behave in an unpredictable way. They do not behave or respond to the physical laws. These electrons can be here and gone the next instant. They exist in infinite probabilities of potential when we are not looking at them. Only when the observer focused their attention to that specific electron,

THE UNIVERSE IS IN YOU

the electron started behaving like matter. Before being observed, the electron acted like a wave, like water when going through the slit. However, when observed, then the electron became and acted like matter. The observer collapsed the wave function of the particle.

This is an important concept to understand and it can be a life changer.

When we redirect our energy and attention into our desire, then the subatomical particles will arrange, take form and give shapes to the same energy we put out there. This means we create our own reality (be aware of what we wish).

It is my observation and realization that "LOVE" governs the quantum field or the universal intelligence, and that is when miracles happen. It can only be reached by calming our mind. In other words, by broadcasting signals after elevating positive feelings and having a clear mind, we can create a field of extraordinary energy, attracting anything we can dream on.

As a doctor, I venture to say that it is love that controls our autonomic system, including heart rhythm, breathing, digestive system or homeostasis (temperature, pH or concentration of glucose).

The universe will always manifest our thoughts and synchronize the frequency of our song. Uni-Verse (one verse). This is the reason we need to keep positive thoughts to see positive results.

We are not bound by the reality of the physical plane or physics rules.

Another strange phenomenon in the quantum field is "entanglement". It can be explained as two particles (matter) existing in two different locations, but when one particle is manipulated (we do something to it), the other particle responds instantly. It is like the same particle exists in two different locations at the same time. The scientific world cannot explain why this happens. The theory behind it is that either the information travels too fast to each other or both particles are connected to each other (entanglement). If entanglement is the case, it allows me to think we are all connected to each other from the beginning of existence.

To know the basis of how the quantum field works, it is crucial to monitor our thoughts, mind and feelings. We have more than 80 billion neurons in our body and those cells release incredible amounts of energy through synapsis and electrochemical reactions to each other.

Some research shows that negative thoughts, including depression and hostility are related to high levels of body inflammation. I see it in my daily neurological practice. It doesn't matter what I do with some patients (using either traditional western medicine or the more holistic and natural approach of treatment), their health does not improve because they allow negative thoughts to dominate their mind.

It is well known that chronic stress leads to many diseases, and it is not a coincidence that the majority of people suffer from many internal conflicts like anxiety or depression.

I deeply believe that when we have a thought with a strong desire, the signal and message are formed in a dimension that we do not quite understand, later to form into reality that meets us.

We act like a big antenna, constantly sending signals and getting a response.

Our thoughts are energy, generated by neurons. Each neuron is unique

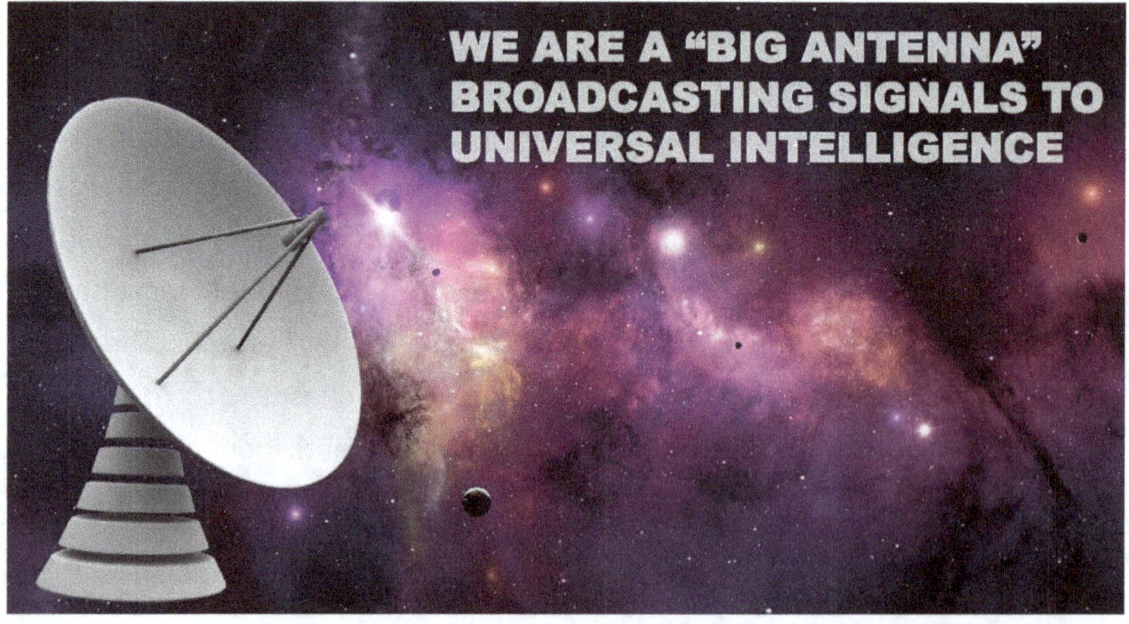

and responsible for information. Each neuron is connected to another neuron through synapsis, and they communicate to each other with chemical signals, called neurotransmitters. Each time you learn or create a new experience, neurons are making new connections. This process can change the physical anatomy of the brain.

It is also said that our thoughts could be from a universal field or collective mind.

Everything is energy. There is a vibration of energy around us, and as Einstein said, matching the frequency of that energy creates our own reality. This is the reason we have to have a clear mind to get what we want in life.

The universe is in us.

As humans, we are energy. As we know, energy cannot be created nor destroyed. Consequently, we always exist. We are eternal in different forms.

The physical universe is formed by atoms. Atoms are formed by sub-atomic particles (protons, neutrons and electrons), but are also made by other particles called quarks, neutrinos and many others. Inside the atom is where "energy" resides and some call it "the field of information". What we see as matter is just pure energy consisting of a lot of information with a very tiny amount of matter (99 percent of matter is just energy).

One of the words we always hear is "chi" or "qi." It is the energy current that runs through our body. This energy flow creates a pathway that connects acupuncture points on the body. These pathways between points are called meridians and manipulating these points can help to create better energy flow and help different illnesses by restoring balance in ourselves.

I believe that an imbalance of energy in our body could be the cause of many medical illnesses.

Helping to balance our energy can be done by practicing tai chi, yoga, meditation, reiki or having massage therapy.

It is very important to do what we love to synchronize our own vibration. This is why doing the hobbies we love or being more creative will help

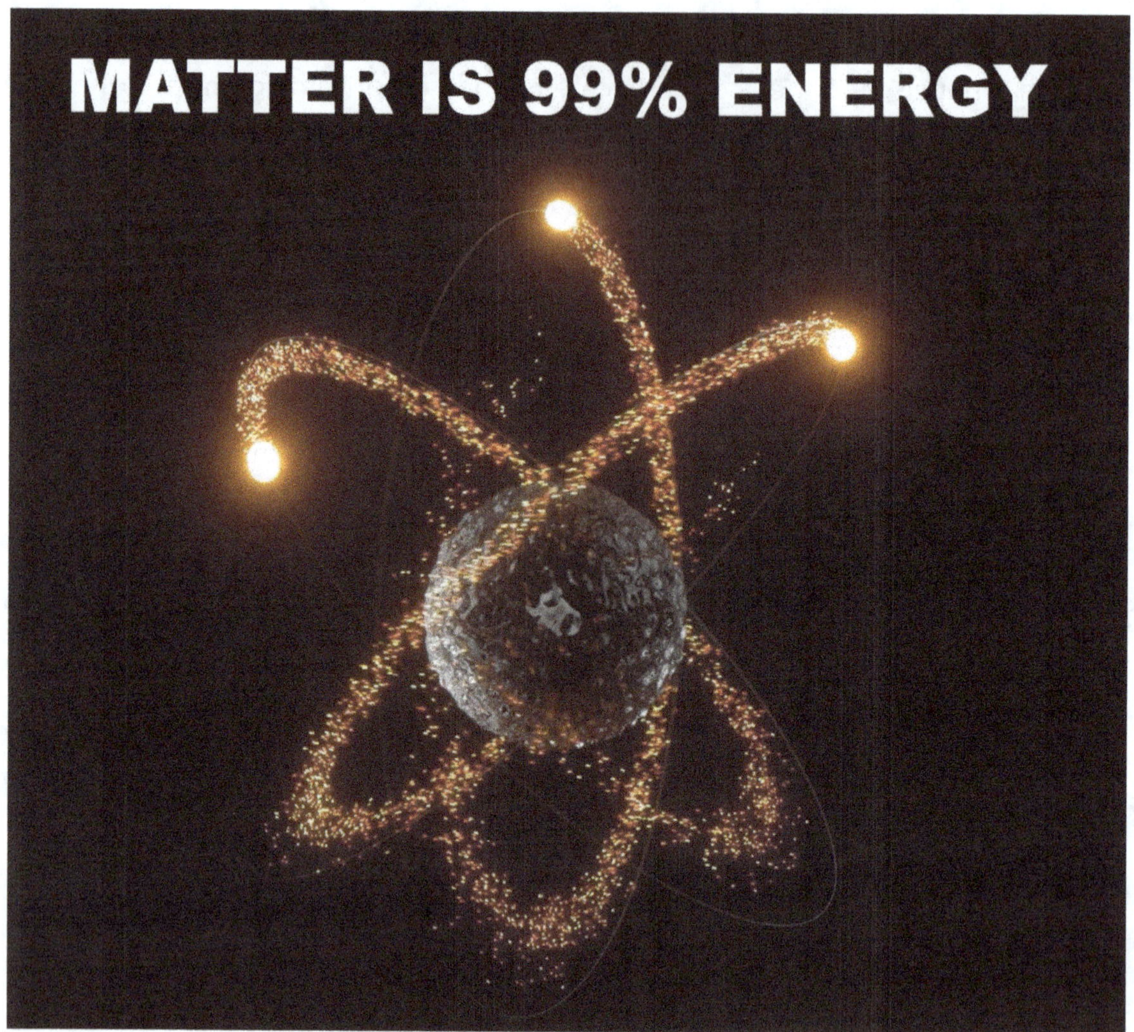

us to be healthier.

We are constantly creating our reality. If we constantly think in our past, then we create what we are thinking. In recent years, a lot has been written about living in "the present." I believe that is a difficult concept for the mind to understand because the mind survives and is nourished by the past and future.

The past is made from our thoughts, which is information we accumulate as we live. The mind always projects what is coming, which is the future (a conceptual state of mind that helps us in the decision-making process).

It is clear that the mind doesn't grasp the idea of "present" since the mind is represented by our history of memories, past experiences, and constant projecting into the future. The past having already passed and the future yet to come, we are constantly living in a non-grounded reality.

Reality is made by our own decisions. If we are not happy with our reality, then we should make better decisions.

We have about 6,000 thoughts per day, and most likely 80 percent of these thoughts will be repeated the next day. It would be considered insane to expect a different reality in the future if we keep thinking the same way.

If we imagine a better future through our feelings and thoughts, then at the quantum field (at the sub-atomical level) that desire will manifest. It is a matter of time. We are in charge of our own reality, stay focused and you are going to receive your desire.

Sometimes I think the process of creation (poetry, music, or a painting) brings us closer to being "in the present" and it is when we release or unleash inspiration, that it becomes the language of our soul (the area of no time). I believe "the present" is no time.

It doesn't matter how many times we go back into our own past; we cannot change that experience unless we use it to see how far we have come.

We are mortal beings when we live in a time and space reality. In the physical plane, we decay but we are mainly made of energy that never dies.

I believe we are spiritual beings; we never die. I do not believe in the state of death; I believe in transformation. All creations in this universe never perish, but are always transforming.

Remember, we are pure energy and energy cannot be destroyed.

I mainly practice geriatric neurology. I treat patients who believe they are dying. I try to tell them that they will never die, but it is a very difficult concept to understand.

When patients ask me my age and my answer is "I do not have an age because I was never born," it creates confusion. Some do not come back to see me because they believe I am crazy.

When they come back, I make sure to tell them how great and young they look (even if they are 100 years old). I also ask then to tell me good news. I say, "I don't want to hear any bad news."

They almost always laugh, which is a good therapeutic way to start the visit. It never fails, the patients who are positive and optimists are in better health.

The ones who are negative and pessimistic are always complaining of the same symptoms or worse and it is very difficult to help them, regardless of what I do.

Believing in your own doctor is one of the best treatments for the patient for the simple reason that believing is very powerful.

I always tell my patients that part of my definition of "depression" is that we have "too much past."

I define "anxiety" as when we have "too much future." If you tell the mind that we should live in the present, it will not understand that concept.

If we removed our attention from the physical world: people, sex, time, religion, race, gender or age - we become nobody, no place, no where. This is when we become closer to being in the "present."

Just remember that every time we refer to "the present," it is an area that the mind cannot conceptualize.

Being in the present, you are no longer identifying yourself with things in the physical world. You are more tuned to the field where no material exists.

We are made of body, thoughts and consciousness. Our body is our physical temple. It is the representation of our genetic expression.

Our thoughts are where we carry all experience from the past toward the future (information). Our consciousness is where our soul resides (the plane of inspiration).

Consciousness is where our instincts, essence and spirituality inhabit at the non-physical or virtual level. When I am at this level, I am free because I do not have to put anything into a specific place or time. This is when I am no-body and nowhere.

Consciousness is to be "aware" and self-awareness is the ability to rec-ognize ourselves as an individual, separate from the environment. Mindfulness is a mental state that is the ability to focus on our own awareness, in the present

WE HAVE OVER 6000 THOUGHTS/DAY

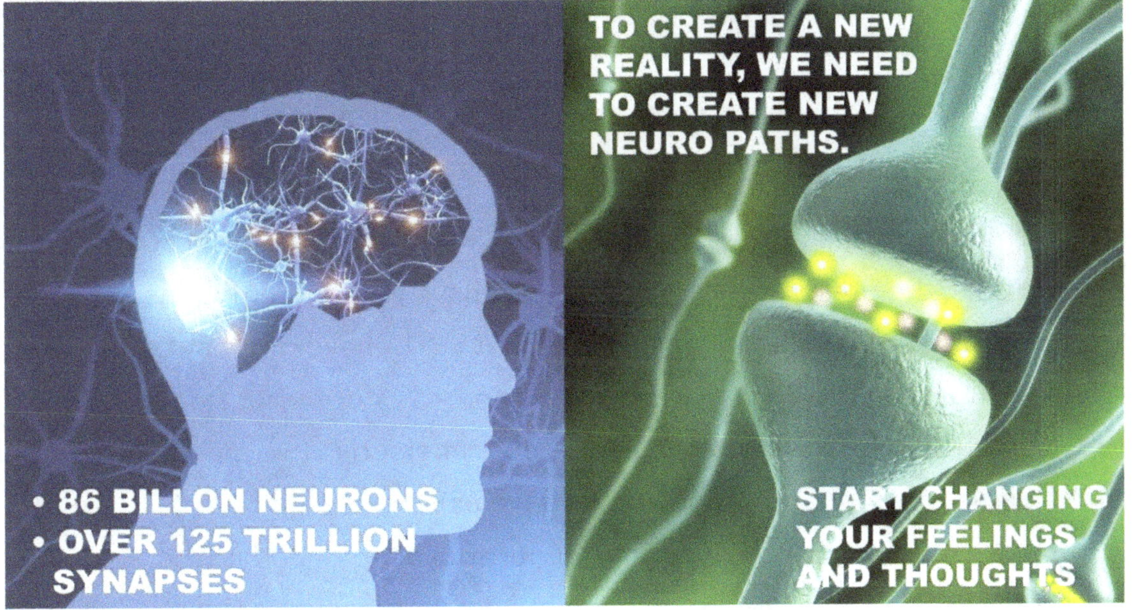

moment, and is used as a technique to calm our mind.

I believe that it is in our consciousness when the natural forces and the source of making the right decisions for our life occur.

When we align our consciousness with thoughts (mind) and body, then we are more balanced and healthier. Enlightenment can then be reached as a state of being. The universe's intelligence is taking care of us. The word "enlightenment" means "into the light" a sense of understanding or being in touch with our inner self. Usually, people seek this stage of being through meditation.

On a personal note, I have found peace when I am doing what I love or staying in a quiet place. Then I feel we are not humans **DOING** any longer, we become **HUMAN BEINGS**. For me, expressing art is entering into my own rhythms.

Sometimes, the reason we suffer is because we allow ourselves to be attached to objects and people. To be free in its fullest, we must release

OUR TWO MAIN ESSENCES

The Brain	The Consciousness
Thoughts	Soul/Spirit
Feelings	Instincts/Creativity

any form of attachment.

The brain is the house of our thoughts, which are the product of our past (from birth to the present time), causing us to have different emotions and feelings, and based on those feelings we are going to behave one way or another. These thoughts can be manipulated, indoctrinated or domesticated by our previous experience from the culture we are immersed in (we are the product of the discipline our parents and school gave us).

The consciousness is the house of our soul or spirit and is where our instinct resides and can never be touched by the human mind or be changed by our social media, is the place without a place, and the purest essence we can possess. It communicates to us by a gut feeling, that is why we should listen to those sensations to make less mistakes in our lives.

FAITH

Faith is a very powerful instrument that we all carry. The reason I mention this is because bringing all of the energy of faith into the "belief" can transform our cells to the point that we become healthier or sicker. It is a complete trust or confidence in something and usually based on any spiritual belief.

Faith helps us in so many ways, allowing us to feel and have more hope when things do not get better.

Negative thinking is another way of having poor faith in positive outcomes.

If we embrace our mistakes and displace the negativity of any events,

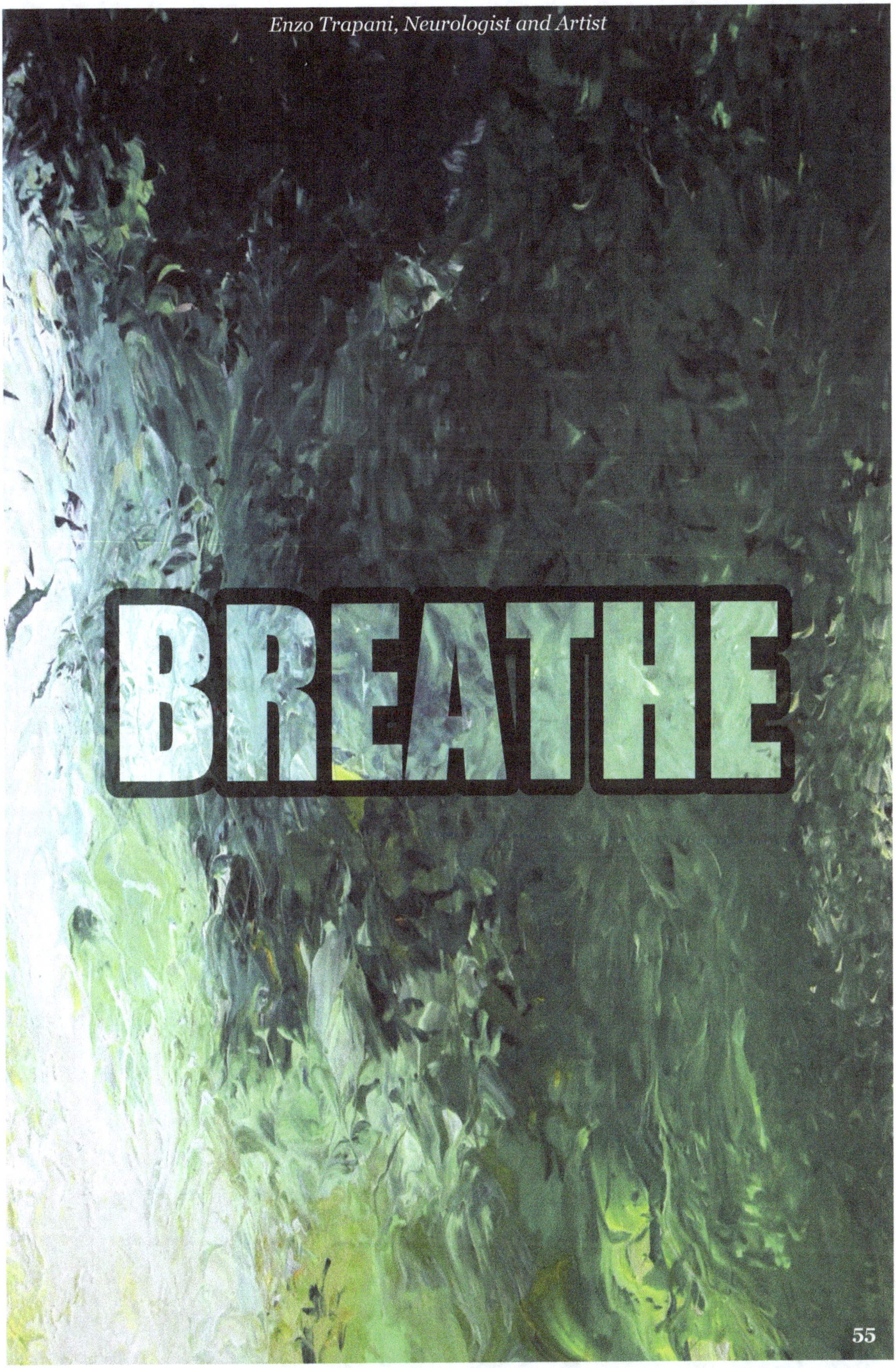

BREATHE

faith allows us to move forward, without getting stuck.

It not only gives us strength and positive thinking, but it gives us real purpose in life, which is important to conquer any desire or wishes, and fear will vanish.

In my medical practice, I observed that people with faith heal quicker.

There are so many scientific studies to support that faith healing really does work.

Some have suggested that healing is a sign of the placebo effect.

If we have faith in ourselves, our high positive energy field can improve and strengthen our immune system, allowing our cells to repair faster in a more natural way.

There is a field called neurolinguistics, which studies the relationships between our language and the nervous system.

The reason I mention this is because we can read and repeat words in a ritual way, which will result in believing and having faith in what we just said.

For example, if we verbalized the following italicized paragraphs, it could help to improve and strengthen our immune system. Just repeat it a few times a day when you feel weak or ill.

"I am connected to a superior plane through my main essence, creating strong molecules, cells, organs and systems, so that no bacteria, virus, parasites or toxic substance can lower my frequency of love and weaken my immune system.

"I command harmony in all my chakras, broadcasting high vibrations of energy in all of my body to create a shield against any exter-nal or internal insult. It will destroy and eradicate any illness, bringing peace and happiness into my existence.

"I believe it is already happening."

I heard or read these words at some point in my own research and travels. They resonated with me and has been part of my own spiritual practice today.

BELIEF

"Belief" is a powerful tool we all possess. The biology of belief (the chemical changes of the cell that occurs as we believe) is the definition of "placebo." Knowing that the mind and body are "one"   we realize that our inner chemical make-up changes based on the way we feel.

A fascinating event in human psychology is when we can have multiple personalities. One of the personalities could have an allergy to a specific medication, while the other will not. This condition will help you to understand the power of the mind.

In my own experience, when I see patients with a terminal illness, I learn that sometimes the "diagnosis" of something terrible like "cancer" will kill you faster than the cancer itself. Under the knowledge of a bad diagnosis, our body becomes immunosuppressed and less resilient to the cancer cells. I do believe that we die sooner knowing something bad is going to happen.

I also believe that one of the most important words in our vocabulary is gratitude, to say "thank you"   Sending these vibrational words to the universe can create a different biological make-up in our body. It will lead us to a better state of health.

A very common experience during my practice of neurology is when I hear a statement such as "Doctor, I have severe arthritis and low back pain," or "I am too old for this or that."

Realize how powerful words are. The moment we said it, we became what we said, slowing down the natural process of healing. Words are very powerful and we become what we think or say. This is the reason why sometimes monitoring our thoughts can help us to be more aware of our state of mind.

It is well proven that if we start thinking differently or we have different experiences, we create different brain connections and could change our brain structure, leading to a new reality.

If we keep doing the same thing or not changing habits, our neuronal connections will create the same reality and nothing will change.

The only possible way to be more complete or become happier (when we are not happy with ourselves) is if we start to feel, think and act differently. We are a conditional brain machine, that with every daily thought, we create a chemical chain reaction that allows us to feel and act the same way we did in the past.

The secret to break that chain reaction is if we start living and experiencing different thoughts. In essence, we have to monitor our own thoughts to become more aware of what it is we need to change.

LOVE

It comes to mind how I should define "love." For thousands of years, and after many definitions, "love" is an intense feeling of deep affection. It's a direct state of emotion toward something, somebody or ourselves.

However, if we define "love" in a more universal way (the supreme intelligence or the source), then we will realize that it is all around us, like the fabric of the universe. When we direct a specific love to something, we always need an important ingredient which is "passion" or "compassion"

Without either of those, we would be like a bird without wings, we would not be completely free.

When we feel an individual love, such as to a person or a thing, there is a chain reaction which can lead us to compassion, forgiveness, joy, acceptance, allowance, peace, and happiness. When we have the opposite of love, we feel arrogance, envy, insecurity, frustration, rage, jealousy and hatred within us.

Love is healing for the simple reason that it has a positive vibration energy.

Love is a natural state of being.

It has positive energy and the highest frequency of vibration, creating good proteins and health.

Do what you love with passion, be honest with your feelings, meditate, have faith and enjoy the now.

LIGHT IS THE MOST POWERFUL SILENT MUSIC

I feel we came to this life to learn, have joy and pass your experience to others. We have to have some degree of love to be attracted to something, and that "something" in the material world has colors.

While it sounds very appropriate and correct to make the statement that body and mind are "one," we need to be honest with ourselves. Our thoughts have to be aligned with our intention, which will mean we will exist in a more harmonic state.

For example, let's say we want a red Ferrari or a healthy body, then we imagine that specific car in front of the door or a well fit body. To be more powerful, we need to add an emotion to that concept, which means "we feel that specific desire already happened."

The power of the imagination is a very strong energy that allows us to conceptualize our own desires. It is the bridge between the past and future and that is how we construct the pathway. If we do it right, then we can become our own genie in a bottle. Behind any desire, we need some degree of effort or discipline to reach our goal.

The Enzology Formula

In my formula, I said that love is light since it is the source of all the creation in the universe. Love without light, love will not exist. Without love or light, life will not be possible around us. Love and light are always entangled or fused.

I also mentioned that having a positive environment, will enhance our own love and light, making us healthier.

Our environment is all around us, from our internal environment, which is our thoughts, and our external environment, which is the place we live.

Light is color, that is the reason that love has all the color of the rainbow.

The three positive energies that make us healthier are love, light and environment.

With a positive attitude, we experience pleasant and happy feelings. This brings us more energy and happiness. Our whole being broadcasts good

Enzology formula

LOVE= [LIGHT] EV⁺

ENVIRONMENT

will, happiness, and success. Health is affected in a beneficial way.

Positive and negative thinking is contagious.

We affect and are affected by the people we meet, in one way or another. This happens instinctively and on a subconscious level, through words, thoughts, feelings and through body language.

WE BROADCAST THE WAY WE THINK. Negative thoughts, words, and attitude create negative and unhappy feelings, moods, and behavior. When the mind is negative, poisons are released into the blood.

POSITIVE THINKING CONTRIBUTES TO HEALTH BENEFITS that can decrease depression, stress, improve cardiovascular health, increase life span, and overall better well-being.

OUR UNIVERSE

Intelligence is all around us, inside the dry rock or in us. We are intelligent beings.

Every time we talk about the universe, it is almost impossible to avoid the question, "When did everything start?"

If we believe in the Big Bang Theory, then it all started 13.85 billion years ago. It may be at that time that light (photons) was born.

Philosophers and physicists do not like the idea of nothingness. That could be one of the problems with the Big Bang Theory because from nothing to becoming a universe cannot be explained in the physical realm.

To believe in the Big Bang Theory, we have to prove this phenomenon started from a specific time and place, and so far, that cannot be determined or scientifically explained.

In General Relativity, the Big Bang is a spacetime singularity; meaning as you go backward in time, you eventually run out of time, or out of "spacetime."

It is difficult for our mind to understand that beyond 13.7 billon years ago, there was no time or space and that means the universe has always been here because there was no time before 13.7 billon years. In other words, there was never a time when the universe didn't exist.

Therefore, we do not have an exact theory how everything starts and the origin of the universe.

When it come to us, I can say that we are made of the same elements of the universe and the universe is in us. We can manifest our own reality because we are the creator.

To create and manifest our reality, we need to focus positively and align our intention. If we believe in ourselves, take action, work on it, visualize and have positive thoughts, then we will cultivate positive feelings and manifest our dreams.

Epigenetics and the Secret of Living Longer

EPIGENETICS is the study of heritable changes in gene expression that does not necessarily involve changes in the DNA, but involves the way the chromosomes affect a gene's activity and expression.

Perhaps we remember from high school that DNA doesn't change. The environment may not change the sequence of the DNA, but can change the expression of the genes or the gene activity (genes can be "on" when they should be "off" or vice versa).

An amazing discovery is that these changes we carry in our own DNA can be passed through generations. In a simple explanation, epigenetics show that DNA expression can change based on the environment in which we live. This concept allows me to see the medical field from a different view.

Before explaining DNA in a scientific way, I would say DNA is a structure inside the cell and produces proteins. This structure will change for good or bad based on the environment in which we live. Good environment will generate good and healthy protein for our body. *This is the main concept of Enzology™ and to understand Pill on the Wall®.*

Taking into consideration this concept, I will explain the basics of cell morphology at the DNA level.

DNA (Deoxyribo Nucleic Acid) is a long polymer made of repeating units or molecules called nucleotides.

Polymer is a large molecule with many units. It comes from "poly" meaning many and "mer" of monomer—small molecule. DNA is a long molecule that contains our unique genetic code (stores all our biological information). Like a recipe book, it holds the instructions for making all the proteins in our bodies.

DNA is made of two nitrogenous bases: PURINES (adenine and guanine) and PYRIMIDES (cytosine and thymine), and they are the building blocks of both DNA and RNA.

In all species, DNA is composed of two helical chains around the same axis.

DNA is mostly located within chromosomes in the nucleus of each cell, but some are found outside the nucleus (in the mitochondria).

Humans have roughly 23,000 genes.

A gene is a distinct stretch (portion or a segment) of DNA that has the blueprint of the production of protein and gives us our physical appearance. DNA-GENES are the protein factory in our body.

Genes have information to build and sustain the structure of cells and to pass the genetic trail to offspring.

Proteins are large macromolecules (amino acids form polypeptides and polypeptides form proteins). We have a lot of proteins in our body. For example, HEMOGLOBIN is a protein inside the red blood cell that has the property to transport oxygen from the lungs to the rest of our body cells.

Also, enzymes are proteins that are used to speed up the rate of many chemical reactions. For example, pepsin is an enzyme that is produced in the stomach, and it is one of the main digestive enzymes that break down proteins for better digestion.

All of our genes together are known as our genome.

The genome is the entire set of genetic instructions found in a cell.

So, we have 46 chromosomes in every human cell, 22 pairs are autosome and one pair is the sex chromosome.

Different living things have different shapes and numbers of chromosomes. A donkey has 31 pairs of chromosomes, a hedgehog has 44, and a fruit fly has just 4.

The environment can switch genes on and off, changing the gene activity. Identical twins are born with the same DNA will have a different genetic makeup in sixty years. They will have the same chromosomes, but their life and environment experiences will be different, causing the switching of their own genes' activity on and off. This causes the DNA to have a different profile and expression.

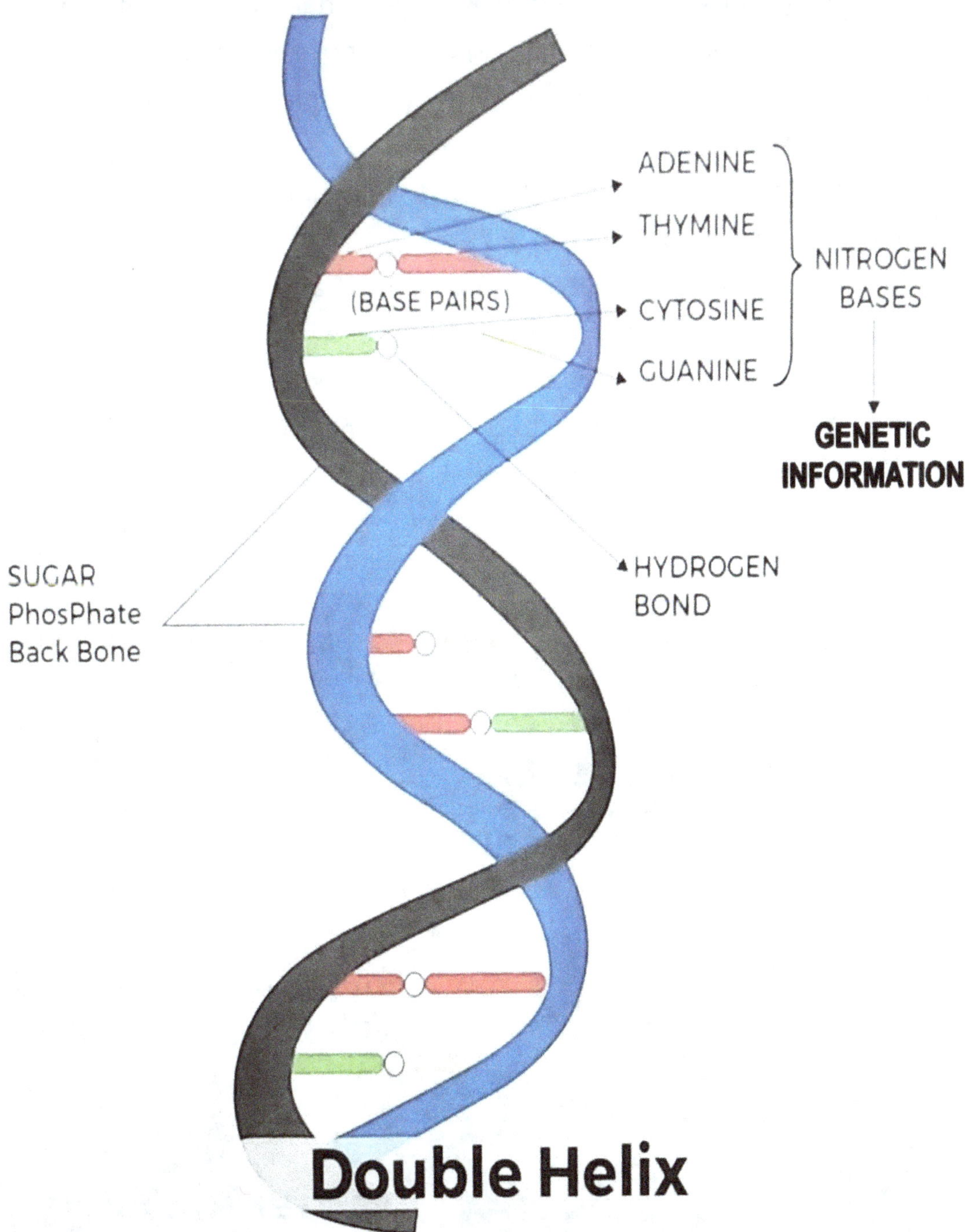
DEOXYRIBO -NUCLEIC -ACID
ADENINE
THYMINE
NITROGEN
BASES
(BASE PAIRS)
CYTOSINE
GUANINE
GENETIC
INFORMATION
HYDROGEN
BOND
SUGAR
PhosPhate
Back Bone
Double Helix

Our environment is made of all our surrounding experiences including our nutrition, lifestyle, emotions, places where we live and work, land, water and weather.

Regarding cancer, epigenetics plays an important role, since it is the environment that turns on tumor-promoting genes (those are the genes allowing cancer to form) or tumor-suppressing genes (genes that slow down or stop the progression of cancer).

In other words, we would like to keep tumor-suppressing genes ON all the time to avoid having cancer.

It is important to know that a vast majority of cancers are non-hereditary. This is the reason that the environment we choose to live in will contribute to developing tendencies to have cancer or other illnesses or not contribute.

We all have a great potential to prevent so many illnesses if we are aware of the importance of the environment we are in.

Cancer is likely to occur due to a mutation of the DNA causing the gene

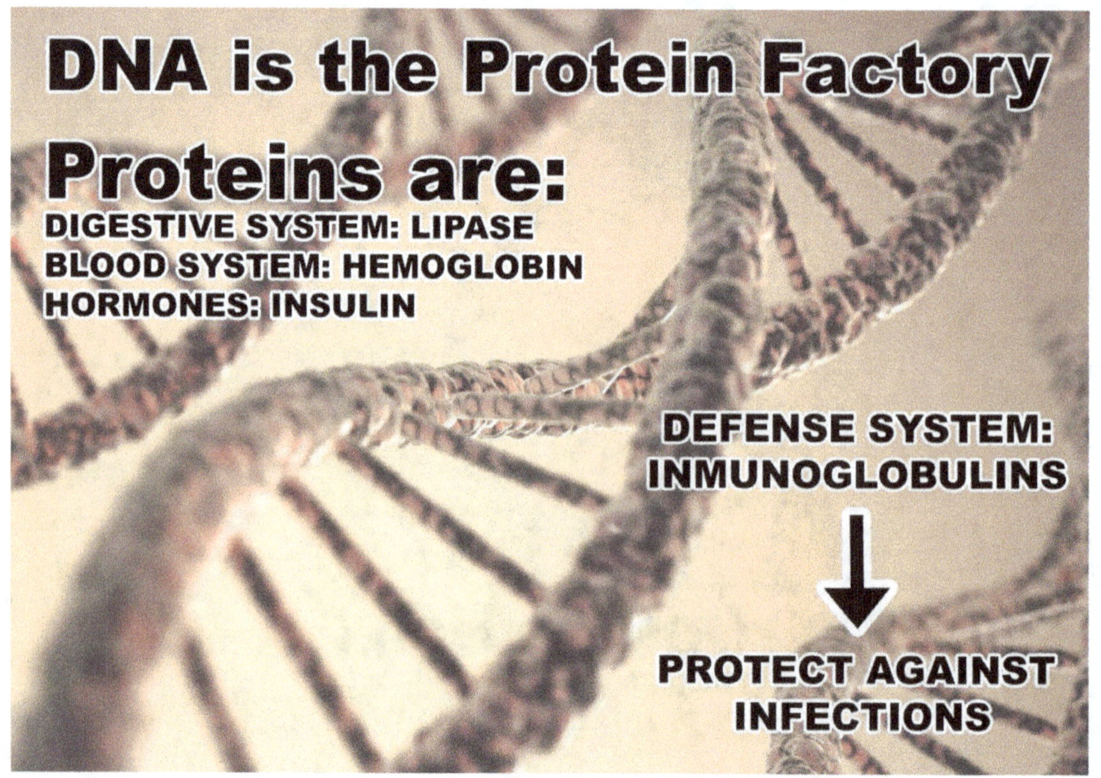

to give the wrong instructions inside a healthy cell, then the cell will grow without control. Gene mutation normally occurs in a normal cell, but a healthy cell has a mechanism to recognize this mistake. If this mistake is missed, then it could become cancerous.

As I have explained to my patients, we are all born with tendencies to develop specific illnesses in our body. If we choose to live an unhealthy lifestyle (smoke, drink lots of alcohol, lack of exercise, obesity, poor nutrition or living in a toxic emotional environment with lots of stress), then we may increase the risk of developing that specific illness.

I mentioned cancer since it is one of the main causes of death, but coronary artery disease (heart attack) and strokes are the leading medical problems causing death and are important to prevent. As we know, the risk factors for these conditions are high blood pressure, diabetes, lack of physical activity, obesity, smoking regular cigarette and high cholesterol.

LIVING LONGER

The secret of living longer has been studied for centuries and a child born today will live a life span 20 years longer than one born in the early 1920s.

Now, we have basic knowledge of human cells. We know the DNA is located inside the chromosome (in the nucleus) and the genes are a portion of the DNA, and the genes are the protein factory of our body. Also, we know the environment can change the expression of the DNA, making us healthier or sicker.

Next, we need to know about something else inside the cell, in the DNA, called telomeres.

Telomeres are caps at the end of each chromosome and an essential part of human cells, protecting the chromosomes during normal cell division. They protect the chromosome from damage.

In a normal cell, each time a cell divides, the telomeres become shorter. Eventually, telomeres become so short that the cell can no longer divide, resulting in the inability for the DNA to be copied any longer and the cell begins

HUMAN CELL

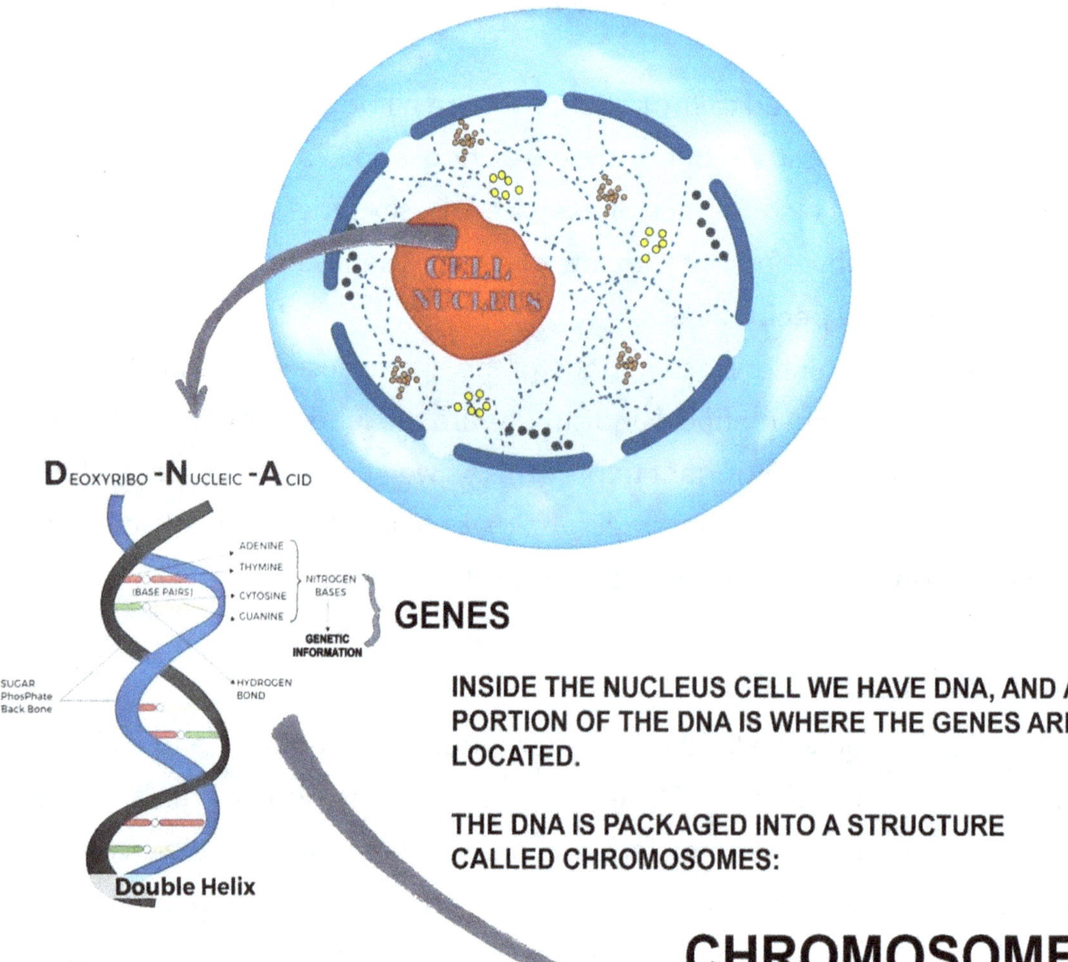

INSIDE THE NUCLEUS CELL WE HAVE DNA, AND A PORTION OF THE DNA IS WHERE THE GENES ARE LOCATED.

THE DNA IS PACKAGED INTO A STRUCTURE CALLED CHROMOSOMES:

CHROMOSOME

WE HAVE

23 PAIRS OF CHROMOSOMES = 46 CHROMOSOMES
22 PAIRS ARE AUTOSOME (NO SEX CHROMOSOMES)
1 PAIR IS A SEX CHROMOSOME (XX FOR A FEMALE, XY FOR A MALE)

to age and can no longer replicate.

Telomeres hold the secret of longevity.

Over the course of a lifetime, as cells divide, telomeres become shorter, leaving chromosomes (the house of the DNA) vulnerable to damage.

Not only does normal aging shorten the telomeres, but life stressors over time can cause similar effects.

I believe this further proves the environment plays an important role in our aging.

Aging is not just genetic, but the lifestyle we choose to live.

An enzyme was discovered to repair and maintain these telomeres, and is called telomerase. This discovery led to a Nobel Prize for Medicine in 2009. Studies showed the level of telomerase was higher in younger people and levels dropped with age.

It is clear that telomeres shortened as we aged, but lack of exercise, poor nutrition, chronic smoking and increased amounts of stress contributed to this decrease.

Shorter telomeres also are associated with many medical illnesses, including diabetes, hypertension, depression and cardiovascular diseases.

When we are highly stressed, the sympathetic nervous system (the autonomic or involuntary system that regulates important body functions such as heart rate, sweating, pupils, digestion, blood pressure, and more) hyper reacts and the brain sends signals to the adrenal gland, releasing cortisol.

STRESS = increased CORTISOL

Cortisol is the main "stress hormone" in our body and is released during the "fight-or-flight" response; but it plays an important role in regulating blood pressure, body sugar (glucose), keeping inflammation down, regulating body metabolism and much more (controls sleep-wake cycle, salt-water balance and assists with memory formulation).

When we are under too much stress, increased levels of cortisol are released causing anxiety-depression, headaches, fatigue-lack of energy, trouble sleeping, memory problems, premature aging, depressing our immune system, digestive problems and high blood pressure.

Certain adrenal gland tumors produce too much cortisol leading to a condition called Cushing syndrome (causing weight gain, diabetes, high blood pressure, fatigue, memory problems, bone loss, acne and many other health problems).

Some stress can be good, keeping us alert and motivated, but too much stress can cause us to develop physical symptoms like headaches, high blood pressure, chest pain, sexual dysfunction or an upset stomach. Also, it can cause emotional problems like anxiety, depression or panic attacks.

Long-term side effects of chronic stress could cause heart disease, brain stroke, chronic hypertension and depression of the immune system, leaving the body vulnerable to infection or disrupting the digestive system. Chronic stress may cause memory, cognitive and learning difficulties.

One thing we should know is that chronic stress could cause overproduction of cytokines. Cytokines are proteins produced by cells that play important roles in our body, such as regulating the immune system and inflammation, repairing tissues and stimulating the production of blood cells.

Chronic stress can lead to the overproduction or inappropriate production of certain cytokines leading to medical problems, including inflammation like rheumatoid arthritis and many other illnesses. Chronic inflammation also increases the risk for heart disease (atherosclerosis), osteoporosis, diabetes type 2 and neurodegenerative disorders (dementia and Parkinson's disease).

It is clear that reducing stress in our life allows us to be in better health and to live longer. Fortunately, there are many ways to decrease stress, live longer and feel better about life.

For many years, the secret of living longer has been extensively studied and numerous researches have been done. It is clear that the broken DNA (our protein factory) leads to cell damage, many illnesses and death.

During normal aging, it comes as a result of multiple factors, not only damage of the DNA, but stem cells exhaustion.

Stem Cells

Stem cells are the fundamental building blocks of life and have the ability to differentiate into different type of cells and repair damage tissue in the body like cancer, infection or injuries. They are the mother cells of our body.

These cells have the capacity to become specialized such as blood, muscles or brain cells. That is the reason we can offer a great promise for medical treatment (regenerating medicine).

There are several sources of stem cells:

- Adult stem cell, from human bone marrow or fat tissues.
- Embryonic stem cells, from embryos that are up to 5 days old.
- Perinatal stem cells, from amniotic fluid and umbilical cord.
- Adult stem cell alternated or genetically modified to have properties of embryonic stem cells

This is very important to know because if we could generate stem cells that could tell our body to produce specific healthy cells, then we could repair damaged cells or regenerate tissues. That is why stem cell therapy could be the right treatment to even improve or cure Parkinson's disease, Alzheimer's disease, amyotrophic lateral sclerosis, type 1 diabetes, leukemia, spinal cord injury, COPD, heart diseases, arthritis, pain reduction, stroke or cancer.

One of the most common stem cell therapies is for bone marrow disease (the bone marrow is the body factory of our own cells, located inside the bone), treating patients with leukemia or autoimmune disorder (autoimmune disorder occurs when the body is attack by its own immune system and danger antibodies target their own body tissue, like lupus and multiple sclerosis) through blood stem cell transplant.

Zombie Cells

Another cause of diseases and our aging is the accumulation of "senescent Zombie cells."

This type of cell normally occurs throughout life and plays an important role in our immunity, wound healing or tumor suppression.

The steady accumulation of these types of cells with aging could lead to cell death. These cells release potentially harmful chemical signals to the neighbor cells, leading to cell damage. It is said that during this process, inflammation and cell damage occurs.

Our body naturally removes senescent cells through a strong immune system.

There are specific drugs that selectively clear senescent cells in our body, and they are called "senolytic-drugs" (Quercetin, Dasatinib, Fisetin and Navitoclax).

These senolytic drugs or supplements are not FDA-approved for this indication yet.

Another important factor on aging and diseases is the ability to generate or produce healthy proteins, known as proteostasis.

Typically, human cells contain up to 20,000 types of proteins. Proteostasis maintains healthy proteins for healthy cells.

During aging or many illnesses, this homeostasis or normal protein production is lost.T o maintain a healthy protein production, it is crucial to exercise regularly, have proper nutrition and a positive environment.

Nutrition

Nutrition is the key, but it is not everything.

When it comes to nutrition, many things can be said, but you can never be wrong eating natural food including fruit and vegetables, and you can never overdo it. I believe eating meat in moderation cannot be detrimental for your health.

I have to mention a very comprehensive study done in recent years. It was called "The China Study'' (the bible of vegans), which took more than 20 years and was conducted by Dr. T. Colin Campbell, PhD. The study included roughly 6,000 people from 65 rural counties in China and examined the link

Enzo Trapani, Neurologist and Artist

THE SYMPHONY OF THE UNIVERSE ORCHESTRATES OUR HEART RHYTHM AND BREATHING PATTERN

between the consumption of animal products (including dairy) and diabetes, cancer, coronary artery disease and cancer.

The study was clear, showing concrete evidence that eating animal-based protein is more likely to cause cancer and heart disease than plant-based protein.

In conclusion, this study advocates eating protein from nuts, lentils, soy, beans or broccoli.

Even if you have all the possible knowledge on nutrition and health, I personally believe that "moderation" is the key when it comes to nutrition.

It is not always about the type of food we eat, but the way you eat it. Eating an organic carrot and watching toxic local news on TV by yourself is more detrimental than eating homemade spaghetti with meatballs on a long table surrounded by friends and family, laughing and spending hours with them. The digestion is better because we are adding a positive environment to our meal.

I will mention more in detail the benefits of nutrition in the Food and Colors chapter.

Exercise

Exercise is a crucial element in life, with so many benefits.

As I tell my patients, exercise and antidepressant medications, like Prozac, have similar effects. By increasing the heart rate, our body will produce more serotonin, which has an antidepressant effect on our mood.

Exercise will not only improve your mood, but much more. Benefits include a decreased incidence of heart disease, improved good cholesterol (the HDL), normalizing your blood pressure, and decreasing the incidence of brain stroke and controlling your weight (losing weight not only improves diabetes type 2, but also decreases incidence of heart disease).

As we do regular exercise, our sleep patterns improve (engaging in at least 30 minutes of moderate aerobic exercises two to three times a week, especially in the morning or afternoon, but not close to bedtime).

Exercise can increase the level of endorphins and keep some people awake. Also, right after exercise the core body temperate can rise, which would cause in some people to be more awake.

It is not clear how the physical activity improves sleep but it is known that moderate aerobic exercise increases the amount of slow wave or deep sleep. Exercise also can relax, decreased anxiety and stabilize the mood.

You can never overdo exercise, unless you have a medical condition that limits your physical activities.

Exercise strengthens our muscles and bones, is healthy for our joints and improves balance. Also, it helps to decrease pain in our joints (helping arthritis) and to improve the circulation in our legs (decreasing atherosclerosis formation).

Exercise can be fun, enjoyable and increasing our socialization in group fitness classes may allow us to connect with friends, which is great for our mood and behavior.

There is clear scientific evidence that regular physical activities (from aerobics to a brisk walk) increase brain volume in the frontal and temporal area, improving cognition-memory.

Avoid sedentarism at all costs.

In my own experience, I feel calmer and experience more joy after finishing exercising.

Physical exercise can definitely regulate stress and anxiety, increasing brain levels of hormones having a positive effect on our mood.

Weight lifting improves muscle mass and bone density, which is very important as we age because, during the aging process we tend to lose muscle mass. Improving muscle mass and bone density will help prevent osteoporosis.

As we all know, inactivity is a major contributor to weight gain, which is another reason to keep active.

Exercise has a positive effect on pain. The majority of my patients, with chronic pain, have sedentary lifestyles and are very inactive.

One of the most common conditions I encounter is fibromyalgia (generalized muscle and joint pain associated with depression) and most of these patients do not exercises on a regular bases. Their main reason not to exercises is because they are in pain, but I try to get them to understand that thinking has a snowball effect on them and leads to more pain. I tell them that simple stretching or a brisk walk can improve their pain.

Chronic low back pain is a very common condition I see in my daily practice and physical activity will increased the pain threshold or raise pain tolerance, decreasing pain perception.

Exercise can improve or stimulate skin blood flow, delaying skin aging.

Moderate exercise can increase the level of HDL (good cholesterol) and lower the level of LDL (bad cholesterol) preventing or reducing the incidence of heart disease and stroke.

Regular aerobic exercise lowers the blood pressure amount for people with hypertension.

I see significant number of patients with cognitive or memory problems, and a majority of them, do not exercise on a regular bases.

Exercise improves brain function, mood and memory, increasing heart rate and promoting blood flow and better oxygenation to the brain.

There are at least five booster chemicals I should mention:

- **Serotonin** is a neurotransmitter that play an important role in our mood. Lower levels of this substance in the brain is linked with depression. Serotonin should increase with aerobic exercises.
- **Dopamine** is another neurotransmitter and is a chemical that gives us motivation. Decreased levels of dopamine is linked with mood changes and neurodegenerative disorders like Parkinson diseases. Exercise can boost dopamine levels in our brain.
- **Norepinephrine** is another neurotransmitter and is increased with high intensity workouts because they stimulate the adrenal glands (the glands that release this substance), becoming more alert, able to focus and improve the ability to concentrate.
- **Endorphins** are natural pain relievers and can boost your mood. This chemical can be produce by your body after exercise,

laughing or sex. Endorphins also are known as endogenous opioids. It is a very familiar experience to have an endorphin rush after a long run or heavy exercises. They give us many health benefits including reducing pain, improving mood, boosting self-esteem, improving pleasure and cognition/memory.

• **Brain-derived neurotrophic factor** (BDNF) is a protein and acts like a fertilizer for the brain. Exercise increase the brain production of BDNF and it may promote new connections between neurons, mainly in the memory center like the hippocampus area, improving cognition. As we know, the most common type of dementia in North America is Alzheimer's diseases and this neurodegenerative disorder cause short-term memory due to lesions or abnormality in the memory center. We lose brain volume as we age and exercise is the most natural way slow down this process. BDNF not only can be increased by exercising, but also through sunlight (vitamin D), weight loss, proper nutrition and socialization. Aging, chronic stress, refined sugar, saturated fat and process food can decreased BDNF.

Bottom line, exercise improves health, prevents many medical illnesses, increases our energy and allows us to live longer.

Meditation

The word meditation comes from the Latin word *meditari,* which means *to reflect.* It is a mind-body exercise or practice that allow us to be calmer and relax, removing thoughts and promoting attention of the present moment.

The most common types of meditation are mindfulness and concentration, but they are different types of meditation. Any meditation requires a peaceful and quiet place. I believed we should practice the one is right for us.

During **mindfulness meditation**, we pay attention to our thoughts, concentrating with awareness and focus on our breathing or an object.

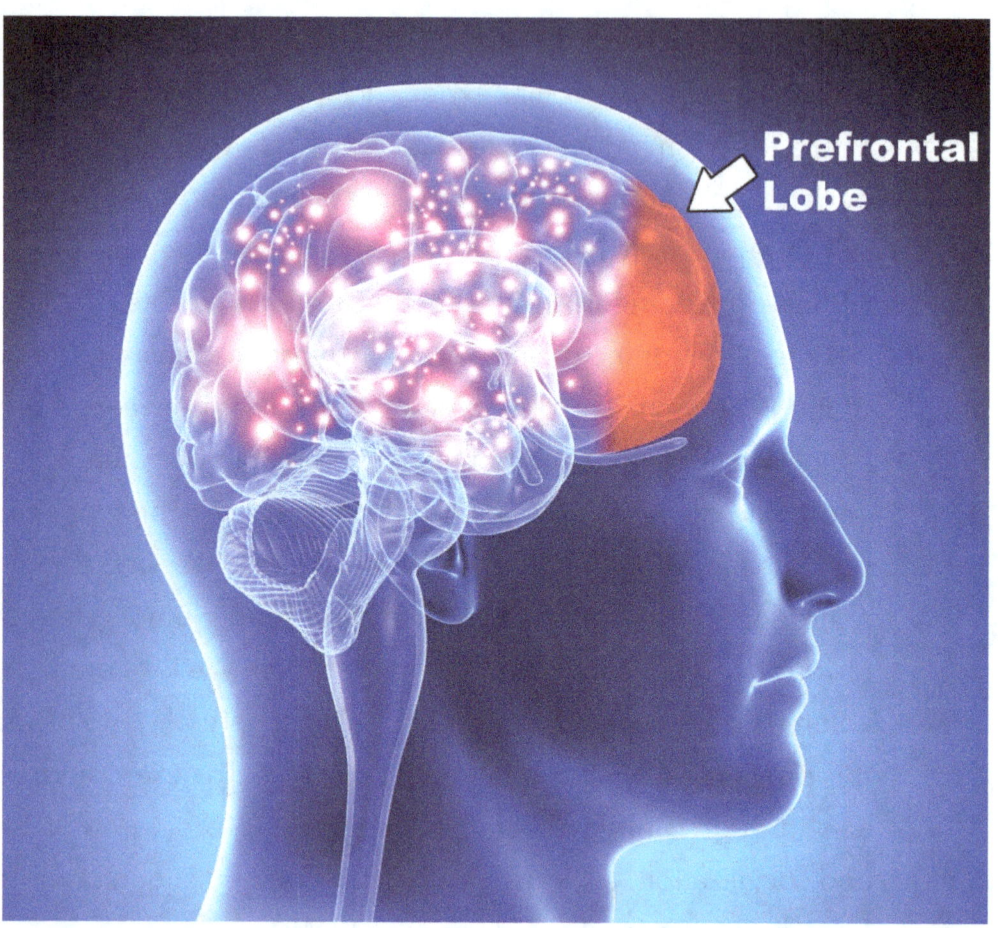

Focus or concentration meditation can be done using something external like a gong (circular metal disc that is struck with a mallet), staring a candle flame or counting mala beats; or concentrating on something internal like our breathing. This type of meditation with help to improve attention and focus.

Mantra meditation. This type of meditation uses repetitive sounds – the most common is "om." This allows us to focus on the sound of the words and decreases distraction.

Spiritual meditation. This type of meditation allows us to be more connected to a high power or any spiritual force. It can be done anywhere or in a place of worship. This practice is good for the people looking for spiritual guidance. A few affirmations can be used to practice spiritual meditation like:

- My mind, body and spirit are in complete alignment with the universe.

- I am a divine expression of the universe.
- My body is a spiritual being.
- I am guided by the power of the supreme energy.

Movement meditation. This type of meditation guides us to be connected with our body thought movement. Ways to do this type of meditation is through tai chi, walking or simply gardening. It is good for people that like to meditate through movement and find peace.

One of the movements that is important to mention is Qi Gong, originated in China more than 3,000 years ago. Qi Gong is a healing practice that combines control breathing, gentle movement with meditation.

Transcendental meditation. Is another technique to quiet the mind, inducing a state of peace. The way to practice is to sit in a relaxed position, close your eyes, breathe normally and chant the mantra inside of you.

Visualization meditation. Is a meditation that focuses on a positive image or scene. Another way to practice this technique is to focus on a matter, or selecting attention on a desired goal to become reality. This type of meditation is used to achieve what you want in the future (envisioning the desired future to obtain desired outcome).

Loving-Kindness meditation. This is a great way to cultivate kindness, sending goodwill and warmth to others. This practice can involve bringing someone to mind who's been kind to you or someone with whom you have experienced difficulties. It helps to promote compassion and decrease resentment.

Progressive muscle relaxation. This meditation is used to reduce muscle tension by becoming aware of a group of muscle that are tense. The way to do it is to tense each group of muscles and hold it for few seconds, then exhale as you let your muscles relax. It helps us to unwind before bedtime.

I recommend to start practicing meditation on a daily bases - few minutes a day is better no time at all. Then, slowly add more time. You determine the limit of how much time you want to spend meditating each day.

The health benefits are incredible and can be achieve in a short time. Meditation can

- Increased focus
- Reduce stress
- Improve blood pressure
- Improve memory
- Boost concentration
- Boost energy (prana)
- Boost creation
- Reduce pain
- Reduce inflammation
- Improve mood
- Increase self-awareness
- Reduce negative emotions
- Allow to be in the present
- Strengthen immune system
- Control anxiety
- Reduce depression
- Lengthen attention span and improve focus
- Improve kindness and empathy
- Improves sleep
- Change gene expression
- Enhance metabolism
- Increase brain gray matter
- Release endorphins.

We always have to deal with stress in our daily lives and as we know, stress increases the levels of a hormone called cortisol. This hormone, in high blood levels, promotes inflammation by releasing chemicals caked cytokines.

Inflammation in our body is linked to so many medical illnesses including heart attack, cancer, stroke, and many others autoimmune diseases.

This one of the main reasons why meditation can help to reduce stress and promote good health.

Reducing stress and levels of cortisol, can decreased the blood level of cytokines, which are inflammatory chemicals that cause multiple medical problems. The overproduction of this cytokines can lead to inflammatory diseases like rheumatoid arthritis or many others infection diseases.

Meditation allows us to align our heart and mind, feeling complete and more connected to our inner self. Our desires and wishes will be materialized if we can reach that state of being, giving us that alignment with our mind and heart. Because it creates positive feelings toward ourselves and then toward others, meditation generates kindness.

Meditation may prolong lifespan. Some studies showed that just doing meditation may lengthen our telomeres (the cup at the end of our chromosomes that have been linked to longevity).

I find it fascinating to know that meditation can change the structure of your brain.

A study done at the Harvard School of Medicine hypothesized that meditation could change the physical structure of the brain (thickness of the cerebral cortex – prefrontal area), which is the area involved with attention, high cognitive function, and the crucial area of the brain involved with problem solving, intelligence and making rational decisions rather than impulsive ones.

Functional Brain MRI can detect increased brain activities during meditation.

Another study of the brain was done with a machine called SPECT (single photon emission computed tomography). It analyzed the brain blood flow during meditation, showing that the prefrontal cerebral cortex (an area of the brain implicated with decision-making, personality expression, planning and social behavior) became more active.

This analysis is telling us that a simple act of meditation could change the chemistry of the brain.

One study showed that doing meditation about ten minutes a day, will enhance attention and memory after two months.

Meditation has an epigenetic effect and can change the expression of our DNA. It means that during the daily practice of meditation, we could generate good and healthy protein for our body.

Meditation is like diving deep into ourselves after pausing our life for minutes, leading into a more harmonic state and peaceful mind. That is the main reason that helps to relieve anxiety and promotes emotional health by removing negative thoughts.

In my daily neurological practice, I see many patients with chronic pain, and I recommend to them to practice meditation because some research suggests that the incorporation of meditation is beneficial for controlling pain, since the perception of pain is connected to your mind.

The bottom line: meditation improve your physical and emotional health.

Keeping your mind busy

I will never forget the patient I saw in the ICU, working as an intern. The patient was close to 80 years old and had a large brain stroke. She was close to being in a coma at the time I saw her. A few days later she was reading the newspaper by her bedside. I realized this patient was a very intellectual person and had an active mind. Always participating in social events, daily reading and socializing will keep your mind active.

How did she recuperate so fast?

I started studying and became more aware of a condition called neuroplasticity or brain plasticity. This is the ability of the neurons (cells of the brain) to grow and reorganize, and make new connections to repair and compensate for damaged cells.

Then, I stumbled into another concept called cognitive reserve which is a protective mechanism the brain poses after having brain dysfunction or brain injury.

LACK OF LOVE CREATES ILLNESS

Let us say, later in life we are going to develop dementia of the Alzheimer type. If we have a great cognitive reserve, the manifestation of this type of dementia will unfold or develop later in life. It would be the same way if we had any type of brain damage; cognitive reserve would give us a cushion to slow down the progression of brain dysfunction.

Genetic and environmental factors will play an important role in keeping a healthy cognitive reserve.

Exercise your mind with socialization and intellectualization reading, participating in different educations and regular physical exercises. This will strengthen memory.

Cognitive reserve is like having plenty of money in a bank account. The more we have, the less chance we have to file bankruptcy. So, if we have brain cell lesions, the good neurons (quality type of neurons that we made stronger with intellectual exercises) can compensate for the bad and injured neurons, so we never go poor or file bankruptcy and we stay smarter longer.

A person who is homeless, depressed, socially isolated, poorly educated or practices poor nutrition is more likely to develop dementia than a person with the opposite lifestyle.

Be aware of the people who surround you

As I mentioned in other chapters, the environment is a crucial element to keep us healthier.

Choosing the right job, partner, friends or daily activity, allows us to be vibrating with the right energy, staying and synchronizing with the natural frequency of the universe. Feeling harmony or inside peace will give us an internal signal that we are on the right path.

Western traditional medicine cannot measure or quantify these energies, but our brain doesn't have to understand everything (like knowing the origin or the beginning of everything). It is important to feel well, especially if we are in touch with our instincts.

Most everyone has had the typical experience of being around somebody and getting bad vibrations from them. We just do not like this person, but we don't understand why.

The reason behind this is that we all constantly emanate vibration (which is energy). This vibration is based on our thoughts and feelings. Happy thoughts create high positive vibration, and negative thoughts and feelings create the opposite.

Negative thoughts make us weaker due to immunosuppressing our defense mechanism (subsequently we get sicker), and the opposite is true when we create positive thoughts.

Just a simple hug can boost immunity. It was reported that people who hug regularly experience less severity of flu-like symptoms.

Oxytocin is also called the *hug* hormone. Hormones can be increased simply by hugging or having a positive physical touch, even if we are hugging or cuddling a pet.

The key is to not surround ourselves with toxic people. They will suck and remove the good in us. If we are depleted of positive energy, we become more prone to physical illness.

According to the life expectancy 100 years ago, you would be lucky to live to 50. By the year 2000, in the USA, life expectancy was 75.

It is also dependent on where you were born. If you were born in a wealthy, positive environment and developed country with great medical care, obviously you will live longer. Babies born today in developed countries could expect to live more than 100 years.

It is true that the place you were born will influence your life expectancy, but it is also true that how we "treat our body" (living poor or rich) will influence your life expectancy.

Knowing the leading medical causes of death allows us to know why we are living longer.

By far, heart disease is the number one cause of death and significant medical improvements in preventing heart disease emerged in the recent years (implementation of internal defibrillator, coronary and many other surger-

DO
NOT
FEAR

ies, also changing nutrition and controlling risk factors like hypertension and diabetes).

The number two cause of death is stroke. Today, with early recognition of the symptoms and proper treatment, we can prevent catastrophic deficits.

Because of advanced medical treatment, the death rate of the main cause of death (cancer, infections, heart or pulmonary disease, stroke) is lower.

As we know, auto or motorcycle accidents are very high in the death rate, but the safety features implemented decrease the chance of death.

We are now more aware of toxic environments, such as sun radiation and pesticides in our food.

Historically, smoking was cool and was used as part of social interaction, but the health department realized that chronic smoking caused more than 480,000 deaths each year in the USA.

It is the first leading cause of lung cancer and chronic obstructive pulmonary disease (COPD).

Smoking also is related to bladder, larynx, esophagus, kidney, oropharynx, stomach, cervix, pancreas and colon cancers. Smoking can clot blood vessels and lead to stroke and heart attack.

Just being more aware about all these factors allows us to prevent future illnesses.

When conversing with my cardiologist colleagues, I explain that the main cause of myocardial infarction (heart attack) is not all related to vascular disease or clotting of the arteries. It can be related to a negative or toxic emotional state.

In other words, we have a broken heart. That is a difficult pill to swallow, especially for a educated professional with logical and predictable reasons in the medical field as to why a person suffers a heart attack.

Sometimes, the reason we suffer is because we allow ourselves to be attached to objects or people. To be free in its fullest, we must release any form of attachment.

I believe that any attachment is always transient and sooner or later we end up losing the object (person or any material object we are attached to).

Everything in the universe is in constant change (anything in existence even the weather) and if we try to hold on it, then, we are going against the natural force, consequently, we will suffer after the loss, leading to anxiety or depression. The root of suffering is holding onto feelings that will not last.

I believe that true joy or happiness is from inner peace and not from external reason or excitement. Nothing last forever. Just as the bad times we may be experiencing will change.

The cessation of all suffering had been called nirvana. One way to reach the state of nirvana is if we can experience enlightenment, which can be reached through meditation, allowing us to be in the present moment.

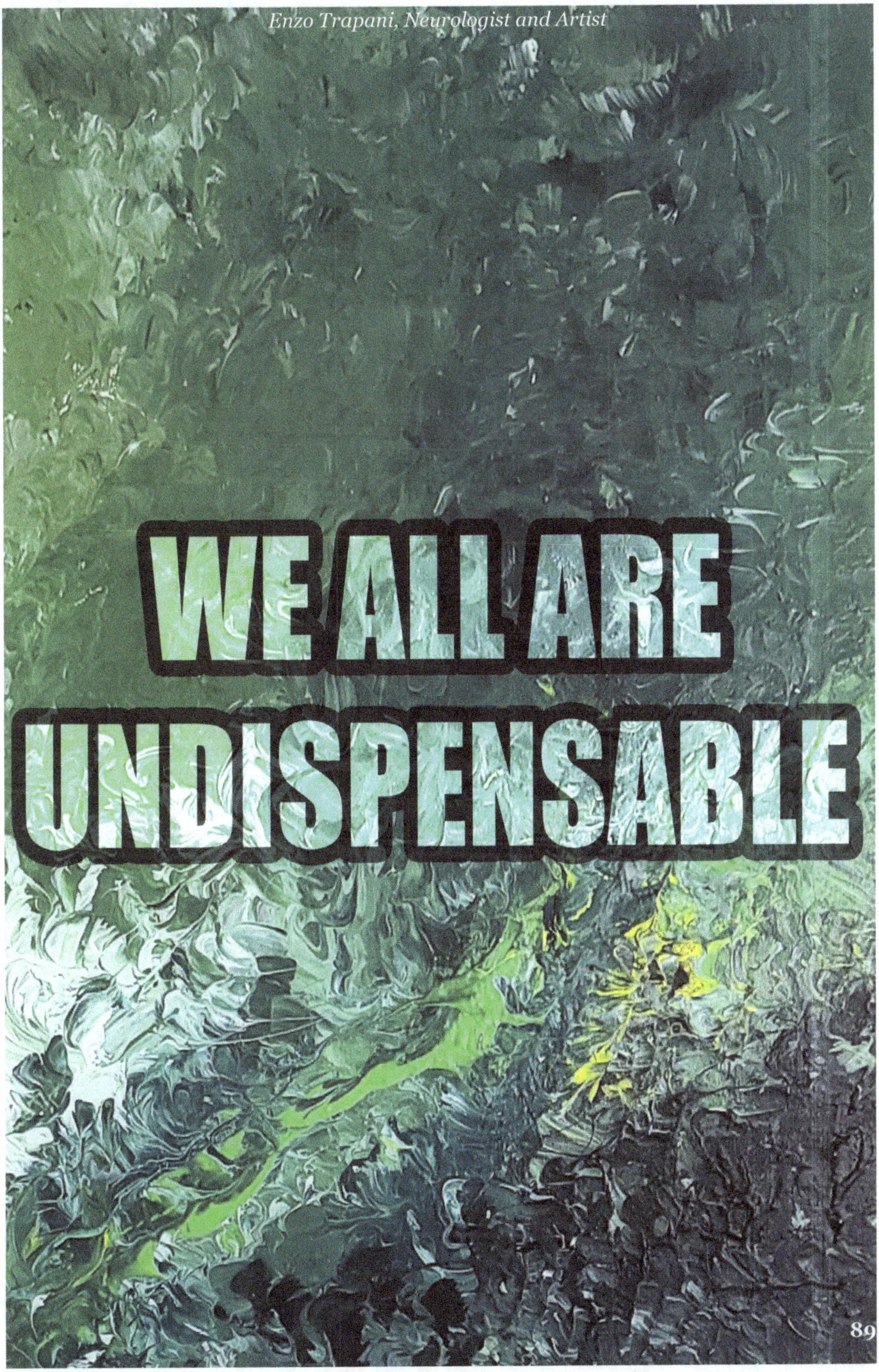

WE ALL ARE
UNDISPENSABLE

Food, Colors and How to Lose Weight

Eating the rainbow is another way to reach our state of being. The different colors of vegetables and fruits are full of nutritional values. The relationship between color and nutritional value has been well researched. The color of the food represents the phytochemicals (phytonutrients) or the plant nutrients in the food.

Yellow and orange colors are very rich in vitamins C and A. Green fruits and vegetables are rich in vitamins K, B and E. Purple produce, like grapes and cabbage, are high in vitamins C and K.

The reason I mention that eating with color is important is because our visual input is as important as our taste perceptions. Even early civilizations like the Romans recognized that we "eat with our eyes."   An astonishing amount of the foods we eat is processed with color that was added to make it more appealing. It is like cosmetics in the food.

Our taste buds play a very important role in our taste (sweet, sour, bitter, and salty) and before we taste the food, our eyes send signals to the brain, getting the flavor BEFORE the food reaches our taste buds. First, we taste with our eyes.

Food companies have researched this concept for a long time, and that is the reason an intense red apple looks more appealing based on our consumer behavior. There is no way we are going to eat blue salmon or drink black water.

It's important to understand a little bit about micronutrients and the relationship between the color of food and nutrients.

Micronutrients are minerals and vitamins. One that is becoming very popular is the phytonutrients phyto refers to the Greek word for plant).

Phytonutrients are natural chemicals produced by plants and have anti-oxidant and anti-inflammatory properties.

There are thousands of phytonutrients and some of the most common are carotenoids, lycopene, ellagic acid and flavonoids.

CAROTENOIDS: There are more than 600 types (beta-carotene, lycopene, zeaxanthin, lutein).

They act as antioxidants and may prevent proliferation of cancer cells. It brings out the red-orange and yellow colors in the fruits and vegetables. The body will convert these carotenoids into Vitamin A, helping with the immune system. Rich in carotenoids are pumpkins, carrots, red peppers, tomatoes, apricots, sweet potatoes, dark green leafy vegetables, romaine lettuce, cantaloupe, broccoli, peas, and squash (butternut).

Lycopene is linked to lower prostate and stomach cancers and protects against heart disease. It gives the pink and red color of grapefruit, tomatoes, and watermelon. Also, rich with this phytonutrient are guavas, papaya, asparagus, mango, carrot, sweet red peppers and red cabbage.

Lutein, Zeaxanthin: These phytonutrients give the orange or green color to vegetables. One benefit is that they may prevent macular degeneration and cataracts in the eyes. Foods rich with these nutrients are spinach, collards, kale, asparagus, broccoli, leafy greens, brussels sprouts, avocados and green peas.

ELLAGIC ACID has antioxidant properties (removes toxins and protects against free radicals). In plants, it also protects against infection and pests. It may prevent cancer and has anti-inflammatory properties.

It is found in most of the berries (strawberries, blackberries, cranberries, raspberries), grapes, pomegranate, guava, pecans and walnuts.

FLAVONOIDS are abundant in plants.

There are several types of flavonoids including flavanols, flavan-3-ols (catechins), flavones, isoflavones, flavanones and anthocyanins.

Flavanones are known for their anti-inflammatory properties, found in

HEALTHY
FOOD
PURIFIES
YOUR
THOUGHTS

lemons, limes, oranges and grapefruit.

Anthocyanin may protect against heart disease and cancer; may slow down signs of aging; found in most of the berries, red grapes and plums.

Isoflavones may lower risk for heart diseases and osteoporosis, found in peanuts, soy and legumes.

Flavones: Are the pigments in the blue and white plants, may protect plants from harmful insects; known to be anti-inflammatory and found in red peppers, parsley, peppermints, celery and chamomile.

Flavonoids have several health benefits including antioxidant, anti-viral, anti cancer, anti-allergic and anti-inflammatory properties. They may also reduce the incidence of heart diseases by lowering cholesterol. They are abundant in red wine.

Green tea is rich in catechins (flavan-3-ols) and has multiple health benefits. It may prevent gastrointestinal cancer, decrease cholesterol, boost immunity, delay aging and enhance rate of metabolism helping to lose weight and may control diabetes mellitus (due to the alkaline nature).

PHYTOESTROGENS are plant-derived compounds. They can exert estrogen-like effects and may interact or alter our hormones.

Often referred to as "dietary estrogen," these compounds are believed to prevent conditions associated with estrogen deficiency, such as osteoporosis or menopausal hot flashes.

In alternative medicine, they are used as prevention against hormone-dependent cancer (breast cancer), heart disease, and osteoporosis. They may prevent endometrial, colon, and prostate cancer.

Food rich in phytoestrogens are soy, sesame seeds, oats, leafy green, garlic, flaxseeds (rich in fiber and omega-3 fatty acids), alfalfa, barley and red clover (used to ease menopausal symptoms).

RESVERATROL is a natural phenol. A great amount of resveratrol is produced in the skin of grapes to protect the plant against bacterial and fungal insult. Therefore, a high concentration of resveratrol is found in wine. One of the wines with higher concentration of resveratrol is Pinot Noir.

It may be important in acting as an anti-aging, antioxidant, and anti-inflammatory. Phenol may also reduce heart disease.

Foods rich in resveratrol are red grapes (skin of the grapes), peanut butter, dark chocolate and blueberries.

When we leave a piece of metal outside, it will rust or oxidize. The same can occur within our cells and could cause health problems. We always have oxidation in our cells. This natural process can and will cause health issues if we do not provide our body/cells with antioxidants.

Vitamins C, E, Manganese, selenium and carotenoids and most of the phytonutrients all have powerful antioxidative properties.

WATER

One of the most important elements in our body is water. Water makes up to 70 percent of human body weight, a loss of less than 5 percent leads to dehydration and a loss of 15 percent can be fatal. Water affects all facets of life on our planet and without it, life on the planet cannot be sustainable.

Water is composed of two atoms of hydrogen and one atom of oxygen (H20).

Some important ways water helps our body are regulating body temperature (via perspiration), protecting body organs, creating saliva, lubricating joints, carrying nutrients and oxygen to cells, helping digestion and flushing out waste products and keeping healthy skin by hydration and boosting energy.

There are studies showing that alkaline water (especially ionized water) compared to acidic water carries more health benefits.

Alkaline water may improve absorption of minerals like calcium and magnesium and may help esophageal or gastric reflux. Reflux disease is typically associated with an excessive reflux of the stomach fluid (acid food, drink,

94

bile and pepsin) into the esophagus and up to the pharynx.

We are always talking about keeping a good pH in our body.

Potential of hydrogen (pH) is a figure or scale expressing the acidity or alkalinity of a solution, on which 7 is neutral. Lower values are more acidic and higher values more alkaline. Our body is always working to control and keep a stable pH. Our normal body pH is between 7.35 and 7.45, which means that the blood is naturally slightly alkaline.

According to the Mayo Clinic, an adequate daily fluid intake is 15.5 cups of fluids a day for men and 11.5 cups of fluids a day for women (fluids are from water and food, usually 20 percent is from food).

Promoting an alkaline state in our body is said to boost your overall health and reduce your risk for chronic illness.

Foods that carry a high dietary acid load include red meat, cheese, soft drinks, refined sugars and many processed meats and grains. Conversely, fruit and vegetables have a low dietary acid load.

It is important to eat citrus fruits. They are acidic, but are considered alkaline because they have a low PRAL potential renal acid load, a measure of the amount of acid your body diet produces).

I believe that eating red meat, cheese, yogurt and dairy products can have healthy benefits, but it is the quantity of these foods that matter most.

FREE RADICALS

During the normal, natural body function, oxidation occurs at all levels (since we need oxygen to survive). During these normal metabolic functions, we create "free radicals" (by-products) as we detoxify.

These free radicals are atoms or molecules with an unpaired electron (unstable atoms) searching for other molecules to collide with so they can steal another electron from them. This changes the structure of the normal molecules, causing abnormal cells and sometimes changing the structure of DNA or proteins.

Free radicals can be originated from our own body (during normal metabolic oxidative function) or from the outside environment (tobacco, food, drugs, air pollutants or radiations).

This is the reason that "free radical scavengers" (antioxidants) should protect and avoid this bad chain reaction.

Our body produces natural antioxidants, but FOOD becomes a crucial way to neutralize free radicals.

Oxidative stress in our body is associated with many illnesses, accelerated aging or neurodegenerative diseases.

Free radicals have been linked with many medical conditions including cancer, Alzheimer's, Parkinson's, amyotrophic lateral sclerosis (ALS), multiple sclerosis, diabetes, arthritis, and heart disease.

We can reduce free radicals by eating less processed foods, stop smoking, avoiding sugar, reducing exposure to chemicals and synthetic products, in-

HOW ANTIOXIDANTS
WORK AGAINST FREE RADICALS

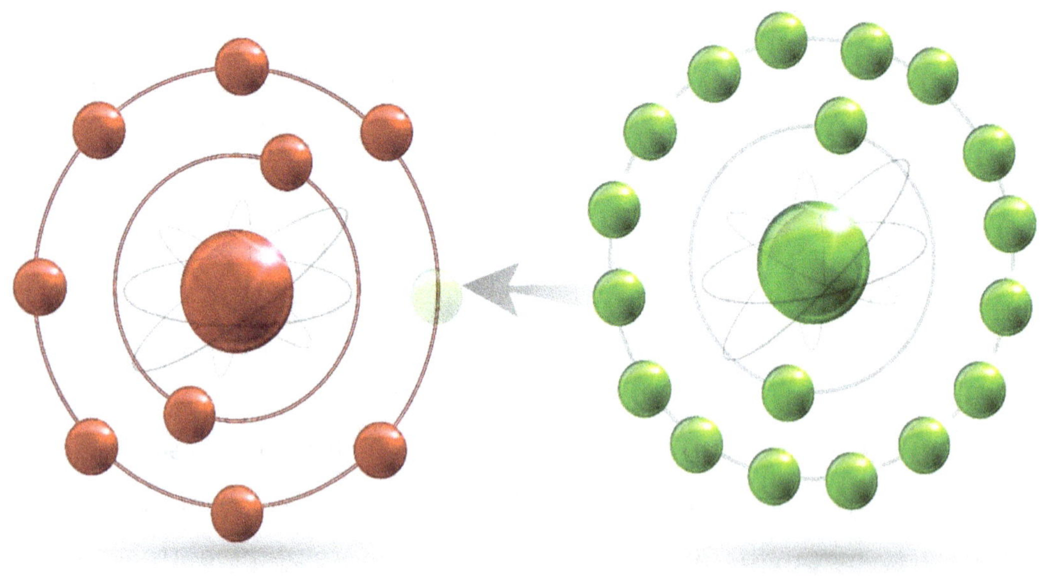

creasing exercise and reducing stress (which may increase free radical production).

To clarify, antioxidants eliminate free radicals by donating or giving an electron to the free radicals and these free radicals become a stable molecule with the paired electron.

In modern society, we are addicted to inflammatory foods, including high refined sugar, salt, fat (processed vegetable oil) and processed food with low content of fibers. All this leads us to a high incidence of diabetes type 2, cancer, high blood pressure, heart disease, obesity, and stroke.

FREE RADICALS ARE CAUSED BY

SMOKING   **STRESS**   PROCESSED FOOD

ALCOHOL   AIR POLLUTANTS

REFINED SUGAR   X-RAYS

REFINED CARBOHYDRATES

ALL ARTIFICIAL TRANS-FATS

One way to increase the level of antioxidant is with positive thinking and meditation. Had been proven that these two habits could increase level of a powerful antioxidant in our body called glutathione.

Also, we can enhance the level of glutathione by eating organic produce such as asparagus, avocado, garlic, spinach, broccoli, cabbage and eggs.

In a clinical study, the use of intravenous glutathione had a positive effect in Parkinson's disease, decreasing tremors and rigidity.

THE COLOR IN OUR FOOD

GREEN

Kale, sprouts, lettuce and broccoli are rich in isothiocyanate and indole. They could prevent cancer (Indole 3 -carbinol may prevent the development of many cancers).

Dark green vegetables are rich in dietary fibers and vitamins A, E and C. These dietary fibers (soluble and insoluble) are the bulk of the plant's food that the body cannot absorb. These unabsorbed fibers normalize the bowel function, helping constipation and lowering absorption of sugar and cholesterol by regulating bowel movement.

ORANGE

Oranges carry beta-cryptoxanthin which prevents heart disease.

Carrots, squash, pumpkin and sweet potatoes have Carotenoids (beta-carotene) which convert into vitamin A, helping the immune system, bone growth and improving our vision.

ORANGE/YELLOW

Oranges and peaches are rich in beta-cryptoxanthin which may help to prevent heart disease. Beta-carotene is found in oranges and grapefruit and is converted to vitamin A, which helps us to maintain healthy eyes and mucous membranes.

RED/PURPLE

Berries, plums and beets are very rich in flavonoids (anti-oxidants).

Lycopene is a carotenoid found in tomatoes, red carrots, watermelons and grapefruit: helps prostate health and could prevent cancer.

RED

Tomatoes and watermelon are high in lycopene, a powerful antioxidant

OUR BODY IS IN PERMANENT HEALING

that prevents cancer and heart disease.

BLACK

Coffee has been linked to being rich in antioxidants and may reduce the risk for colon cancer and Parkinson's diseases.

Onion or garlic contains a high level of allicin and it may prevent heart diseases and lower cholesterol (the "bad" one, LDL). Studies have shown that allicin has antimicrobial properties as well.

Why is the immune system so important?

During my training in medical school, we learned about different systems in our body including the neurological, endocrine, cardiovascular, renal and gastrointestinal, just to mention a few. However, we never learned about our **HEALING SYSTEM**, which I think is the director of the big symphony orchestra in our complex body.

The **IMMUNE SYSTEM** is the system that identifies the threats like bacteria, parasites and viruses, and can kill tumor cells.

The main factories that are responsible for the production of immune cells are the lymph nodes, spleen, thymus and bone marrow, but the white blood cells are the first ones to respond during infections.

To have a healthy immune system, **WE NEED A HEALTHY GUT.**

In the gut, we carry good bacterial FLORA like Bifidobacteria (regulates level of bacteria and modulate immune response), Escherichia Coli (involved in production of vitamin K and keeps bad bacteria in check) and Lactobacilli (involved in vitamin production and protects against carcinogens). We also carry the bad bacterial FLORA (Campylobacter, Enterococcus Faecalis and Clostridium Difficile).

I must clarify the difference between probiotics and prebiotics. Probiotics are foods that contain live microorganisms, to maintain a normal microflora in the intestine.

To keep a healthy balance of bacteria in our gut, we need **PROBIOTICS.** Probiotics are live microorganisms. They are good bacteria, which keeps a good bacteria balance in our digestive system.

The probiotics improve the ability to digest food and to reduce incidence of yeast infections and inflammation. They also increase the ability to synthesize vitamins.

Vitamins are very important nutrients and are precursors to enzymes, which all cells require for a normal function. Humans cannot produce vitamins, so we have to consume from outside sources, like food. But probiotics lactobacillus and bifidobacterium) can facilitate and supply vitamin K and B (cobalamin, thiamine, riboflavin, pyridoxine and folates).

Probiotics can be found in cheese (some cheese can be the source of probiotics, especially if they are made from unpasteurized milk since the pasteurized process kills the probiotics benefits), some yogurts, buttermilk, Kefir (fermented dairy of goat's milk), Kimchi (Korean dish made by fermented cabbage), sauerkraut (fermented cabbage), Miso soup (fermented paste made from barley and soybeans), pickles, Tempeh (grain from fermented soybeans), and Kombucha tea (fermented tea).

Now, prebiotics are foods (typically high in fibers) that act as food for the intestine microflora, they allow your gut bacteria to produce healthy nutrients.

Food rich in prebiotics are garlic, onion, leeks, asparagus, bananas, oats, flaxseeds, apples, seaweed, raspberries and cocoa.

The study done by Masashi Yanagisawa, at the University of Tsukuba in Japan, establish a relationship with poor sleep pattern and depleted microflora in mice (due to lack of production of serotonin from tryptophan).

Food to improve your mood

In general, more whole and less processed food in best for our health.

Fast and convenient food with the combination of sedentarism is lethal.

It is very common to reach for sugary and high calorie food when we are feeling down, but that rash and quick effect in your mood is not healthy at all.

When you're feeling down, it can be tempting to turn to food to lift your spirits. However, the sugary, high calorie treats that many people resort to have negative consequences of their own.

In the United States, antidepressant medication is one of the most commonly prescribe medication, so the question is can we do it in a more natural way, with nutrition.

Many studies had been done and show that specific food can boost your mood because they will affect the level of neurochemical or neurotransmitters in your brain.

Vitamins and minerals can help your mood

Vitamin B6 can increase level of serotonin helping post-menstrual depression (BMJ-1999)

Vitamin C improves mood, according to a 2013 clinical trial in *The American Journal of Clinical Nutrition*. It improves the use of dopamine and serotonin, which are essential neurotransmitters, in our brain.

Folate can improve the mood, according to Dr. Drew Ramsey, author of *Eat to Beat Depression and Anxiety*.

Selenium is a mineral, important for our health and good antioxidant. Can elevate the mood and improved anxiety. According to Journal of Nutrition, 2014, people with low level of selenium, have depress mood.

Vitamin D deficiency had been associated with depression according to Psychopharmacol Journal, 2011.

Zinc, another important mineral playing a role in DNA and the growth of cells, deficiency also was associated with depression, according to the 2017 article "The Role of Zinc in Mood Disorders" in the *Neuropsychiatry Journal*.

WE ARE IN CONSTANT EVOLUTION FOR PERFECTION

Magnesium also plays a role in our mood, according to Dr. Ramsey. He wrote in a PLOS ONE article that snacking on almonds and cashews or eating more spinach or black beans can prevent a deficiency in magnesium. Low magnesium levels could lead to depression.

Foods can improve your mood

Fatty fish like salmon, anchovies, sardines or tuna are great source of omega-3s. Seeds and nuts are sources of plant-based omega 3 fatty acid. Fatty acid is great for brain health and may lower the risk for depression. (*Journal of Clinical Medicine*, 2016).

Fermented food is crucial in the production of serotonin in the intestine (*Behavioural Brain Research Journal*, 2015) because a large percentage of this neurochemical is produce by the bacteria in the intestine. Great fermented foods are yogurt, Kombucha, sauerkraut and kefir. These foods are the reason that healthy guts, lead to healthy mood.

Berries are high in antioxidant, clinical studies (*Nutrients Journal*, 2017) show that the consumption of flavonoids is associated with decreased risk of developing depression.

Dark chocolate with high concentration of cocoa had shows to have a positive effect on memory, mood and inflammation. Could improve blood flow in the brain (*Nutrition Review Journal*, 2013). Important to eat dark chocolate, 70 percent or more cocoa, to avoid eating lots of sugar with high calories.

Oats are excellent source of fiber and can stabilized blood sugar levels, helping your mood. Great way to start in the morning. Eating green oat (Avena Sativa) showed positive effect on mood and cognitive function (*Nutrients*, 2020). Important to eat organic oats and natural and not enriched with sugar. Oats is considered superfood and helping to secrete proper level of serotonin, crucial to keep you in good mood.

Green tea is a great antioxidant and according to a Japanese study published in the *America Journal of Clinical Nutrition*, two to three cups of green tea a day can reduce depression symptoms in the elderly. May be due to a mood-boosting nutrients called L-theanine.

Oysters may have mood-boosting benefits due to the large amount of zinc that can help on anxiety.

Dark leafy greens like spinach and Swiss chard have high content of magnesium, a mineral can help for anxiety. Avocado, almonds and lentils are also great source.

Yogurt is a great source of protein, nutrients, and a fabulous probiotic. As we know, good bacteria in your guts, not only is good for digestive health, but can also boost mood (Psychiatry Advisor, 2015).

Beans and lentils are great source of fibers and plant-based proteins, high in vitamin B, zinc, selenium and magnesium, all good to improve your mood, increasing level of vitamin B12 may help the production of dopamine in the brain.

Seeds and nuts are great source of healthy fats, zin, selenium, magnesium, fibers and plant-based proteins. May help the production of serotonin, like cashews are rich in tryptophan, a neurochemical that your body turn into serotonin.

There is an important system we ignore or we are not aware it exists. It is called the **enteric nervous system** (ENS). This system is the gut-brain connection and is crucial to understand because they are linked with each other.

Information travels back and forth between the two through a vagus nerve. This nerve controls messages that are sent to many other organs in our body, like the lungs and heart. That is why the gut is called the second brain.

One of the main productions of neurochemicals, like serotonin and dopamine, is the gut and having a healthy microflora or bacteria, will help not only our mood but many other things like boosting our immune or endocrine system.

I believe the healing system is not only the immune system, but the integration of all the main systems in our body (cardiovascular, neurological, psychological, endocrinal, renal, respiratory and gastrointestinal) encapsulated and organized by the emotional body.

The environment conditions our emotional state, and through epigenetics, changes or modifies our cells for better or worse.

LOSE WEIGHT BY EATING BETTER

I believe that our weight is a balancing act, when we eat or consume more calories than we burn, will lead to weight gain.

That is the reason a successful weight loss program is based on a balance between calorie intake and physical activities.

According to the Mayo Clinic (*Healthy Lifestyle* article, December 2021), weight loss required six strategies for success:

> • **Making sure we are ready.** Coping with stress, peer pressure or the need of professional support.
>
> • **Find inner motivation.** Be accountable to yourself and take responsibility for your own behavior. No one else can make you lose weight.
>
> • **Set realistic goals.** Aim to lose 1 or 2 pounds (0.5 to 1 kilogram) a week, that will require to burn 500 to 1000 calories more than you consume each day, through a lower calorie diet and or increasing physical activity. As an example, 5 percent of your current weight, may be realist to lose. If you are 180 pounds (82 kilograms) that's 9 pounds (4 kilograms).
>
> • **Enjoy healthy foods.** Decreasing calories need not mean giving up taste.
>
> • **Get active.** Regular physical activity is the key.
>
> • **Change your perspective.** This long-term habit should become a way of life.

According to a weight-loss industry statistics in 2021, the United State weight loss industry is a $71 billon industry.

Another important statistic, shows that 73.6 percent of adults in the U.S. 20 or older are overweight or obese. (CDC)

I deeply believe obesity is an epidemic and should be treated as a chronic progressive disease in the U.S.

Obesity is a very complex health problem that is a combination of multiple causes including genetics and behavior. Just a few of the causes, include:

- Hereditary factors-genetics
- Sedentary lifestyle
- Unhealthy diet-nutrition
- Lack of awareness.

Environment plays a crucial role in having a balanced diet and that include oversized food portions, which are very common in well-known fast-food chains.

Lots of food advertising media encourages people to consume unhealthy foods including poison sugary drinks. It is very common to watch false advertising, showing people drinking sodas and feeling happy, with lots of joy or success. That reminds me advertisements 50-60 years ago, showing people smoking a regular cigarette to represent prestige and being cool, when in fact, lots of my patients are showing up in my office with portable O2, respiratory failure, heart diseases and lung cancer due to chronic smoking.

I believed the same will happen with the food industry in years to come when people will be more aware of the harmful effect of the toxins added to our plate by the social media.

Stress plays an important role in obesity because having anxiety and or being depressed, will lead to eating more, increasing cravings and is another way to canalize our energy. There is a relation between the lack of sleep and obesity, the less we sleep, the more tendency we will have to gain weight.

Some medical illness can contribute to be overweight, including thyroid diseases and diabetes mellitus (type 2) could be the end result of obesity.

I believe that the excess of food intake by people is mostly based on internal conflicting emotions.

Some medication will contribute to overweight and in my medical practice is a common cause since antidepressant, antiepileptic and corticosteroids will lead to this condition.

Overall, our body weight is determined by the amount of energy (calories) we expend during physical activity and food intake.

In most cases, is a very simple and straight forward equation, less physical activity and more food intake, will lead to metabolic imbalance, resulting weight gain, with the exception of some genetic or health conditions some people suffer.

Middle-aged men require approximally 2,200 calories per day and middle-aged women need about 2,000 calories per day, to keep a normal body weight.

The two main factors to burn calories are:

- Portion control will reduce intake of calories
- Exercise will burn calories.

Based on research and the principle of Wishnofsky Rule or weight-loss, to lose one pound of fat or body weight per week, we need to lose 3,500 calories per week, equal to 500 calories per day.

As we know, every person's need is different and to have a proper weight-lose program, it is always recommended to consult with a nutritionist or professional who will give you the proper direction.

Here's a list of some typical foods in our daily diets (Source: USDA, National Nutrient Database for Standard Reference, 2006) and their calories:

Banana: 105

Apple: 72

Egg (large): 102

Milk (2%, 8 ounces: one small cup): 122

Orange juice (from concentrate, 8 ounces): 112

Carrots (3 oz, 1 cup): 52

Oatmeal (plain, one cup): 147

Bagel: 289

Beer (12 ounces): 153

Chicken Breast (skinless, 3 ounces): 142

Coffee (regular-black): 2

Cola (12 ounces): 136

Green been (one cup) 40

Hot dog (beef or pork): 147

Ice cream (vanilla, 4 ounces): 145

Peanut butter (cream, 2 tablespoons): 180

Chocolate chip cookie (from package dough): 59

Butter (1 tablespoon): 102

Cheddar cheese (1 slice): 113

Granola bar (with raisins, 1.5 ounces bar): 193

Oatmeal (plain, without salt, 1 cup): 147

Ketchup (1 tablespoon): 15

Bread (one slice, wheat or white): 66

Potato chip (plain, 1 ounce): 155

Potato, medium (baked, including skin): 161

Rice (white, 1 cup): 205

White wine (sauvignon blanc, 5 ounces): 121

Red wine (cabernet sauvignon, 5 ounces): 123

Spaghetti (cooked, enriched, without salt, 1 cup): 221

Spaghetti sauce (marinara, 4 ounces): 92

Ground beef patty (15 percent fat, 4 ounces, pan-boiled): 193

Pork chop (center rib, boneless, broiled, 3 ounces): 221

Pizza (pepperoni, regular crust, one slice): 298

Shrimp (cooked under moist heat, 3 ounces): 84

Tuna (light, canned in water, 3 ounces): 100

No matter how or when your want to lose weight, a good beginning is

GRATITUDE AND GRATEFULNESS ALLOWS US TO BE MORE COMPLETE

limiting the amount of process foods and refined sugar in your daily diet.

According to a *Health Essentials-Nutrition* article in 2018, Cleveland clinic, there are five ways to win the battle with weight loss:

- **Don't skip breakfast**: "If you skip breakfast, you are starting the day on a dead battery," says Ms. Kirkpatrick. Studies show that higher intake of protein in the morning is also essential for squashing craving later in the day."

Great source of protein includes eggs, sprouted toast with natural organic peanut butter, unsweetened yogurt with berries.

- **Eat small meals**, several time a day, up to six-time day, small meals will keep blood sugar level stable, avoiding blood sugar to rise and fall, causing the energy to fluctuate.

- **Exercise in moderation** since you are trying to lose weight and most likely, you are not in great shape. My recommendation is to start slow and build up.

Just walking 30 minutes a day, brings lots of benefits.

Resistance exercise training will increase muscle mass, and make your stronger, overall.

I encourage most of my patients to do some type of physical activities because it will increase energy and improve the mood, bringing more motivation for any type of goal.

- **Eat until you are not longer hungry**, not until you are full. When you start feeling full, which means you start consuming more calories than you need.

- **Be wary of "emotional eating."** When you eat because you are feeling stressed or having any type of emotional conflict, and find comfort in food, eventually this will become a problem because we cover up the turmoil with food. You may need professional help with psychotherapy to resolve the emotional problem.

There are several foods I would like to mention that will keep you feeling full and decrease overconsumption. One of the best ways to feel full is to eat more fruits and vegetables with lean proteins.

The secret to lose weight is not to eat less, but to eat better.

Research shows that people get full by the amount of food they eat, and not by the number of calories they eat.

The real secret is to decrease the amount of fat and increase the number of fiber-rich foods, such as fruit, nuts and vegetables.

To give you an example, one serving (one cup) of macaroni and cheese that is made with whole milk, butter and full fat cheese is more than 500 calories.

However, if you add 2 cups of spinach and diced tomatoes, and substitute the butter and milk for nonfat milk and light cream cheese, this same serving is at least 200 calories less.

You are eating the same amount, but will feel full faster, because you are adding foods with lots of water and fibers.

There are a few keys that make these types of food special: fiber, fat and water content. Most fruits and vegetables have high water volume, making you feel full with low calorie intake.

If we add whole grains, which are high in fiber, it will take longer to digest and you will feel full longer.

Following are foods for you to consider and keep in mind for a healthy and lean body:

The Apple

Apples are high in fibers and water volume, and contain a compound called pectin, which helps to slow down digestion and promote fullness.

Apples contain a high number of vitamins, minerals and antioxidants (antioxidants neutralize free radicals, when free radicals accumulate in the cells, they cause oxidative stress leading to many diseases), which reduce the risk for cancer, diabetes, heart diseases and obesity.

One of the antioxidants important to mention is called quercetin, and some laboratory studies show it has a neuroprotective effect, protecting brain neurons, and also may reduce the risk for brain stroke. It may also help dementia of the Alzheimer type.

Another study shows quercetin may reduce the level of the LDL cholesterol (the bad cholesterol), and this may be due to the number of fibers.

Apples have a high level of vitamin C, which is an antioxidant and boosts your immune system.

Apples lower risk of developing type 2 diabetes.

Consuming apples may lower the risk for lung, breast and colon cancer, due to the antioxidative effects on the cells.

Fibers in the apple help a person feel full for a longer time, allowing them to reduce overeating.

The Banana

Bananas have plenty of fibers, antioxidants and water, making you feel full. Each banana is about 100 calories, made of mainly carbs and water, and contains a small amount of protein with almost no fat.

It has a type of fiber called pectin and some starch. Eating a banana after each meal allows the stomach to empty more slowly, reducing your appetite.

As the banana ripens, the starch turns into sugar (fructose, glucose and sucrose) and pectin and starch decrease.

Bananas are a great dietary source of potassium. A diet rich in potassium can help to lower blood pressure and decrease risk for heart diseases.

Bananas have a decent amount of magnesium, which also improves heart health. It also contains two powerful antioxidants, dopamine (a natural chemical in the brain) and catechins (a flavonoid).

An unripe banana may improve the action of the insulin, which is crucial for our body metabolism.

Lastly, bananas rarely contain pesticides due to their thick peel.

Oatmeal

Oatmeal is incredibly low in calories and high in fibers.

It contains the three original parts of whole grains, helping with weight control, diabetes and arthritis benefits.

One cup of oatmeal has 6 grams of protein, allowing you to feel full for a longer period of time.

The fibers in the oatmeal contain a type of fiber called beta-glucan, which aids in a healthier digestive track. There is a consistent association between this type of fiber and the reduction of the bad cholesterol (the LDL). Other studies showed the benefits of this type of fiber and the antioxidant properties, as well as anti-inflammatory effects.

The vitamins B, iron, magnesium and zinc of the oatmeal have great health benefits.

The Avocado

Avocados consist of up to 72 percent of water and contain 13 grams of monounsaturated fats (healthy fats) with 10 grams of fibers.

Avocados are one the healthiest foods you can eat. It has become a very popular fruit for health-conscious people. It is loaded with nutrients, including vitamins C, K, B5 and 6, folate, E and potassium and contains more potassium than bananas.

The majority of fat from the avocado is called oleic acid (monounsaturated fatty acid), like olive oil and is associated with reducing inflammation and helping to prevent heart diseases.

Avocados are loaded with fibers that contribute to weight loss, reducing spikes of sugar and helping to lower cholesterol (triglyceride and the LDL-cholesterol linked to heart diseases).

They also improve the HDL-cholesterol (the good cholesterol).

Some nutrients such as vitamins A, D, E, K and antioxidants like carotenoids, are fat-soluble. It means they need to be combined with fat to be absorbed better. One study showed that the fat of the avocado can increase the utilization and absorption of these nutrients.

Avocados also are high in antioxidants (lutein and zeaxanthin), which are beneficial to eye health, and lower the risk for macular degeneration and cataracts.

They may also prevent some types of cancer, like prostate.

Avocado may reduce symptoms of osteoarthritis.

Because they are low in carbohydrates and calories and high in fibers, they contribute to weight loss.

Almonds

Almonds are high in protein, fat and fibers, and contain a lot of micronutrients.

Almonds deliver massive amounts of nutrients, including vitamin E, magnesium and manganese. Almonds contain phytic acid, which is considered a healthy antioxidant. It prevents oxidative stress and is a major contributor to decreasing aging and diseases. The antioxidant power of the almond is largely concentrated in the brown layer of the skin (reason to avoid almonds with the skin removed).

Almonds are high in monounsaturated fat, which reduces the bad cholesterol and can lower the risk for stroke and heart disease.

The high concentration of vitamin E lowers the rate of heart disease, Alzheimer's disease and cancer.

Almonds are very high in magnesium, helping to control blood sugar and high blood pressure. This is beneficial for people with diabetes type 2.

In summary, eating almonds reduces hunger by increasing fullness with low carbs, high protein and fibers.

The Bean

Fava beans are high in fibers and protein with low levels of fats and calories. There are about 14 types of beans (black, chickpeas-garbanzo, cannellini, great northern, kidney, pinto, lima, fava, navy, adzuki, mung, soybean, edamame and cranberry beans). Consuming hummus with a creamy chickpea is beneficial.

Beans are high in antioxidants, helping to fight free radicals. Being rich in fiber, beans lower the LDL (bad) cholesterol and help to bulk the stools, reducing constipation.

Because beans are a good source of phytonutrients (they are the nutrients from the plant like carotenoids, ellagic acid, flavonoids, resveratrol and phytoestrogens), they can lower the incidence of colon, prostate and breast cancers.

A half cup of pinto beans has 8 grams of protein, 1 gram of fat and 22 grams of carbs, with less than 1 gram of sugar.

Beans have a significant plant-based protein and they prevent blood sugar from spiking after a meal, which helps people with diabetes mellitus.

Beans are an excellent source of vitamin B and folate (which improves the nervous system), potassium and iron.

Cauliflower

Cauliflower is rich in nutrients with low carbs and high in water content.

It is very rich in vitamin C, which supports immunity, and is crucial for DNA repair. It also contains vitamin K and other nutrients, including manganese, magnesium, phosphorus, potassium and vitamin B.

Cauliflower is abundant with antioxidants, which reduces inflammation and prevents cancer, and may slow the process of aging and protect the nervous system. It has an abundance of fibers, which helps the digestive system.

Since it is rich in fibers, it supports weight management by boosting fullness and delaying the return of hunger.

Whole grains

Whole grains are made up of three components: the germ, the bran and the endosperm.

The bran is rich in fibers, the germ rich in antioxidants, vitamins E and B and the endosperm contains high amounts of protein and carbohydrates.

Most of the time, the grains we buy in the store are refined grains. During the process of the refinement, the germ and the bran portion are removed, leaving only the endosperm. This is the reason whole grains can leave us feeling fullest, since we are eating the fibers with the other nutrients.

Whole grains are beneficial for people diagnosed with type 2 diabetes, because it takes longer to digest and has a more satiating effect.

They also prevent blood sugar (glucose) from spiking in the blood after meals.

They can lower the LDL (bad cholesterol), lower triglycerides, and may lower blood pressure, reducing the risk of heart disease.

Whole grains are a good source of vitamin B, thiamine, riboflavin and niacin, all important for body metabolism.

Yogurt

Yogurts contain probiotics and a high content of calcium, protein and fatty acids, which aid in the digestive system.

Yogurt is known to contain a lot of calcium, which strengthens bones and prevents osteoporosis. It is rich in vitamin B12, phosphorus and magnesium.

Yogurt is important for appetite regulation and weight control, because it is high in protein.

Many yogurts have been pasteurized, which is a heat treatment that kills the beneficial bacteria for the digestive tract.

Make sure the yogurt you eat has effective probiotics (live active cultures like bifidobacterial and lactobacillus). These active bacteria help the digestive

MIRACLES HAPPEN WHEN WE ARE SYNCRONIZED BY THE POWER OF INTENTION

system and improve absorption of important nutrients, which also helps with irritable bowel syndrome, decreasing bloating.

Every time we improve the digestive system, we improve our immune system, reducing the likelihood of contracting many illnesses.

The controversial aspect of consuming a lot of yogurts is when it is high in saturated fat.

Yogurt is high in proteins, which is very filling, and helps with weight management.

Since yogurt is a milk product, it contains whey (a protein) and lactose. Some people have poor tolerance to yogurt (they lack lactase, the enzyme required to break down lactose). This can lead to abdominal pain and diarrhea.

It is best to consume yogurt with a low sugar content. Yogurt boosts a feeling of satiety.

Cottage Cheese

Another beneficial food that is high in protein and low in calories is cottage cheese. It is rich in calcium and it may promote bone strength. Some studies show that it may reduce insulin resistance, making it a beneficial food for a person with type 2 diabetes.

Some brands of cottage cheese have live cultures (lactobacillus), which are known as probiotics helping digestion.

Cucumbers

There are two types of cucumbers: the slicing cucumbers you eat in salads and the pickling cucumbers, which are usually smaller and used to make pickles.

Pickled cucumbers are a great source of healthy probiotic bacteria, which improve the digestive tract.

Cucumbers are low in calories and a good source of vitamin K, essential for blood clotting. They have plenty of vitamin A, helping vision and the immune system. Antioxidants like beta carotene, flavonoids and tannins, help fight free radicals.

They are abundant in fibers, helping constipation and contain a lot of water (96 percent of water), promoting hydration. Cucumbers are rich in lignans (polyphenols found in plants), helping with osteoporosis and some cancers. They are very low in calories and have a high content of water, helping weight loss.

Quinoa

Quinoa is a plant of the chenopodium family. The edible seeds can be consumed and they are another quality food that is high in protein, keeping you full and healthy.

One cup of quinoa provides more than 8 grams of protein. This type of protein has a wide range of amino acids, which supports the immune system and muscle development.

Quinoa is also high in fiber, which reduces the risk for constipation and high cholesterol. It is a great source of antioxidants and vitamin E, which may reduce the risk for heart diseases and certain cancers.

It contains a high source of manganese, which improves our body's metabolism. It is rich in iron, which assists our red blood cells because it allows the hemoglobin to carry oxygen in the blood, supporting energy and cell function throughout the body. It is also rich in magnesium, which is essential in cell function. A low level of magnesium is linked with high blood pressure, heart disease and type 2 diabetes.

Lastly, quinoa is high in folate, a type of vitamin B that may help in certain cancers and depression. It is crucial during pregnancy for the neurological development of babies.

Chia Seeds

Chia seeds are loaded with nutrients and have a very low-calorie intake.

They are rich in omega 3-fatty acids and possess antioxidant properties. Chia seeds are another food source that is rich in protein and fibers, and will help you feel full for a longer period of time.

Because of the high soluble fiber content in Chia seeds, there is a slow absorption of food. This process helps you to eat less calories and increases your feeling of fullness. A high percentage of carbohydrates of the chia seeds is fiber.

Due to the high content of protein (higher than most of the plant food), chia seeds can decrease the appetite and cravings with great health benefits.

Chia seeds have omega-3 fatty acids and eating the seeds with salmon or fish oil can create a good balance of this fatty acid intake, which may lower cholesterol, blood pressure, reduce atherosclerosis (hardening of the arteries), blood sugar levels, and decrease the rate of stroke and heart attack. They may also reduce chronic inflammatory markers (chronic inflammation is associated with heart disease and cancer).

Another benefit is bone health, since chia seeds have a high content of calcium, magnesium and phosphorus.

Raspberries & Blueberries

Raspberries and blueberries are high in fibers and antioxidants. They are considered on the list of the most powerful antioxidant foods, and assist in keeping free radicals under control. They may lower the inflammatory marker, fighting inflammation. Excessive inflammation can cause damage to the wall of the arteries (the endothelium), leading to cardiovascular diseases.

The antioxidants of the berries like anthocyanins, resveratrol and ellagic acid may protect the skin and reduce wrinkling, as well as protect the body from many cancers (gastrointestinal and breast).

These berries may improve blood sugar and insulin levels. They are very high in soluble fibers, which will slow down the digestive track, reduce hunger and improve the feeling of fullness. They are low in carbs.

Black raspberries and strawberries may help to lower cholesterol. Berries are high in vitamin C and manganese.

Prunes

Prunes are high in fibers and packed with antioxidants.

Prunes are simply dried plums. The content of vitamins and minerals of plums and prunes differs slightly, but prunes have more calories, fiber and carbs than plums. They are extremely nutritious with great health benefits.

Very low in calories, one prune contains 30 calories, 8 gram of carbs and 1 gram of fiber. The fiber plays a role by adding bulk to the stool and may increase the speed that waste moves through the digestive system. The fibers and sorbitol in prunes help constipation when drinking prune juice.

Prunes and plums are high in polyphenol, an antioxidant which has positive effects on bone health and reduces inflammation, protecting cells from the damages of free radicals.

Despite that prunes are relatively high in carbs, they do not appear to elevate blood sugar levels. The fibers slow the absorption of carbs after each meal in the digestive tract, allowing the blood sugar to increase gradually rather than having a spike.

Prunes have vitamin K, magnesium, potassium and phosphorus and may reduce the risk for osteoporosis. They also reduce the chances of heart disease and lower blood pressure due to the high content of potassium, fiber and antioxidants.

Green Tea

Green tea is one of the healthier beverages we can drink.

Green tea is rich in polyphenols, which are natural substances with great benefits like reducing inflammation or fighting cancer. It is rich in powerful antioxidants like catechin and contains a small amount of caffeine that could improve brain function (may increase dopamine in the brain).

Another compound it owns is an amino-acid called L-theanine, which is capable of crossing the blood-brain barrier and may increase GABA (a neurotransmitter), which is helpful for anxiety.

These two substances in the brain (caffeine and L-theanine) can have synergistic effects. It may protect the brain from Alzheimer and Parkinson's diseases (two neurodegenerative disorders of the nervous system).

Green tea boosts your metabolic rate, which may contribute to fat burning effects.

As I mentioned, oxidative stress can lead to chronic inflammation which can lead to chronic illness and cancer, and that is the reason antioxidants can help against oxidative damage. Green tea is an excellent source of antioxidants, helping prostate, colorectal and breast cancer.

Green tea may slightly reduce blood sugar levels, helping diabetes type 2 and may help prevent cardiovascular disease due to the reduction of the LDL (bad) cholesterol. It can help us to live longer since heart disease is one of the leading causes of death.

Eggs

Eggs have many health benefits, and are low in calories and carbs.

Egg yolks are a good source of choline (a micronutrient), which is an important substance for our body's metabolism and nerve function. They may contribute to lower body mass and an increased energy level.

The egg yolk is rich in vitamin D, which is important for the immune system and bone health.

Since eggs are high in protein, they assist in weight loss by helping to increase your metabolism rate and energy level. Eggs leave you feeling fuller longer, which is an important factor in weight control.

One large egg (50 gm) has about 78 calories, 6 grams of protein, 5 grams of fat and 0.6 grams of carbohydrates.

Eggs have a great amount of lutein (a carotenoid), which has important antioxidative properties (preventing cancer). They benefit eye health by protecting against macular degeneration, and can also increase the level of testosterone in men.

Eggs are rich in iodine and selenium, which are crucial to synthesize the thyroid hormone. The thyroid gland is an organ that is key to weight management and regulates the body's metabolism.

Eggs may contain a relatively high amount of cholesterol, but they do not have a crucial impact on cholesterol blood levels.

Eating between one and two eggs per day can have several health benefits. They are a great resource to refuel your body post-exercise, due to the high lean source of protein content.

The combination of protein and healthy fat allows us to stay full longer, which is essential for weight loss. Eggs have no sugar content. Because eggs also have very low carbs, they help keep glucose levels in the normal range.

The WHO (World Health Organization) guideline recommends for children and adults to consume no more than 25 grams (6 teaspoons) of free sugar per day, making eggs a great meal to start the day.

In summary, consuming these foods will improve your mind and health. I believe these foods are the "natural medicine" that prevent disease and allow you to live longer.

Help in Numbers

It doesn't matter how much knowledge you have about the importance of weight loss and how to accomplish it, but it still may not be enough to get you there.

Base on March 2022 article in *Healthline*, peer-reviewed online magazine, cited seven places to find support groups and help:

> • **Support groups**: always if better to be with a group of people sharing similar problems or being listen to.
>
> Meetup.com for weight loss or group fitness training.
>
> Support group on Facebook
>
> Overeaters Anonymous is another one.

The obesity Action Coalition is another option, may have a list of groups by state.

• **Clinical-based groups**: professional including psychologist or nutritionist often run these clinic-based groups. Look for "Local support search engine" and will lead you to the right people.

• **Apps: like MyFitnessPal** has a message forum can connect with others. Other apps could be "Fatsecret" allow you to chat with other people and share stories.

• **Commercial programs**: One of the most popular one is WW (formerly Weight Watchers), this program came with a cost but allow you to interact group meeting and at additional cost can received one-to-one support from a coach. Another one is Jenny Craig, along with meal delivery program, offers community-based support in the form of online forums.

• **Online forum**: Involves online support forum, like Bariatric Pal, Obesity Help and 3 Fat Chicks on a Diet.

It is always recommended to consult with your doctor when you start a new diet or exercises program.

• **Bariatric surgery support groups**: check "American Bariatric" to interact in a forum and discuss with other people their experience.

Also, check on Facebook or Meetup.com for a bariatric surgery group nearby. Local medical institution may be offering support group for this procedure.

• **Start your own support group**: Look into the website that is called "The well Project" and will help to set up the rules, place, content, size and the space you need to start. After all, is about having the right motivation and can be done.

THE SOIL

Soil is a mixture of 45 percent minerals, 25 percent air, 25 percent water with 5 percent dead and living organisms (organic materials), making this planet to be alive and is one of the most important natural resources.

It supports animal biodiversity and is essential for domestic livestock and wildlife, providing water to all vegetations. Soil can filter chemicals and other contaminates for the plants.

It is important to know that one of the main reasons we do not get proper nutrition in our food is because of the quality of the soil. The sources of the soil are roots from our plants and the fruit and meat we eat.

Soil is full of microbes, forming a relationship with plants to protect them and provide good nutrients. According to USDA, "one teaspoon of healthy soil contains 100 million to 1 billion individual bacteria alone."

The crops grown from the past were healthier than the crops that are grown today.

Soil is naturally abundant with life and minerals, but this balance is lost during the use of pesticides. Soil feeds the plants and animals, then we eat both of them but with less nutritional content.

Before the modern farming era, the nutrients in the soil were in better balance. Farmers had livestock and the manure was applied to the soil, returning nutrients into the field.

Modern agriculture methods are using pesticides on soil, depleting nutrition and killing the main living organisms that are living in soil. The reason pesticides are used on the soil is to protect crops from pests, fungal and weeds, which prevents potential losses and maximizes more crops produced. This farming also allows crops to grow year-round. Consequently, more produce is sold in supermarkets. We end up eating food from a depleted soil.

In the past 50 years, food has lost significant amounts of minerals, vitamins and nutrients, which were beneficial for our health and our immune sys-

SOIL

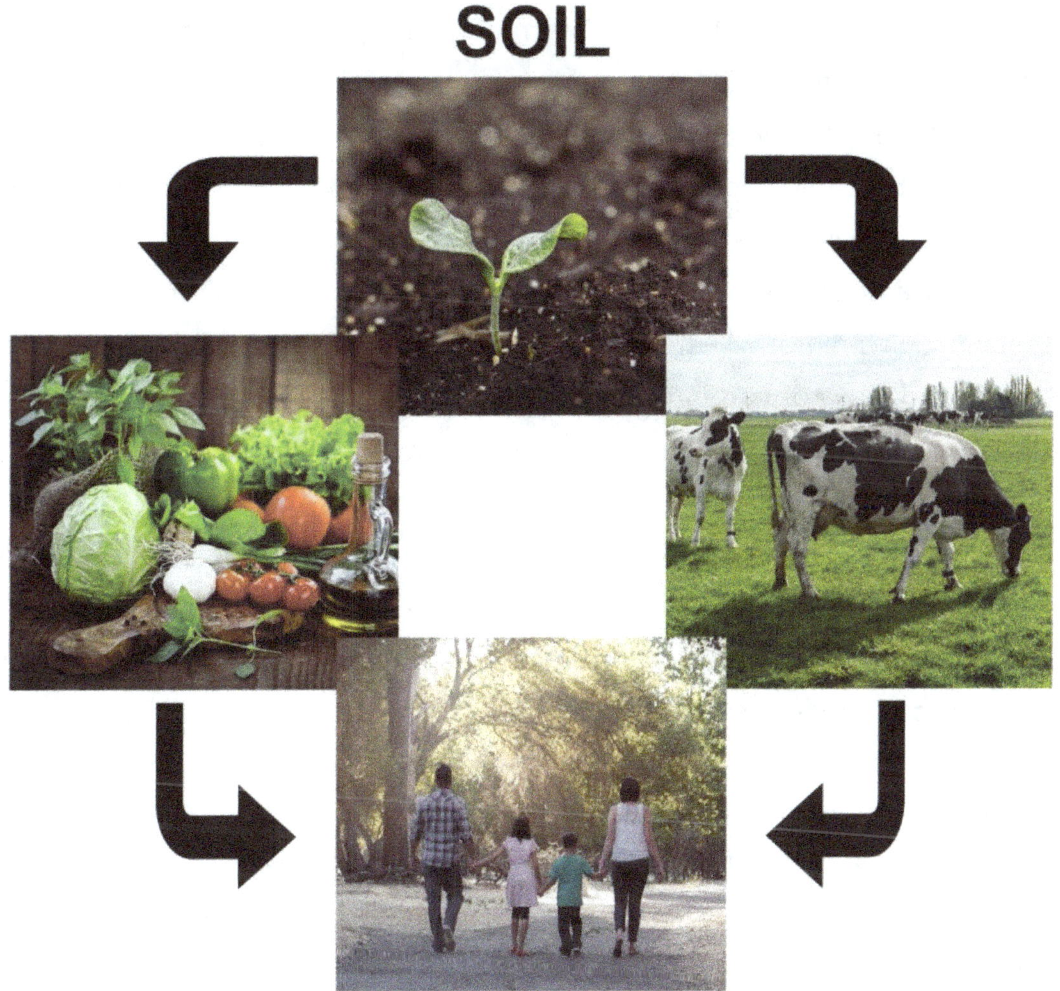

tem. As a result, the incidence of heart problems, cancer and obesity are on the rise.

Animals are farmed with growth hormones and fed with GMOs (genetic modified organisms). This genetic engineering food objective is also used on plants, increasing the food supply in a growing world population.

The problem with adding GMOs to our plates is that the genetic material is changed to our natural food, leading to potential health problems.

Two substances that is frequently found in our food are aspartame and high fructose corn syrup.

Aspartame is a low-calorie synthetic chemical sweetener.

The U.S. Food and Drug Administration (FDA), a trusted source, approved aspartame for the use in food and drinks in 1981. According to the FDA, more than 100 studies have shown aspartame to be safe for most people.

Not to be confusing, but the information and knowledge we have will differ base on the sources we read.

Aspartame is a synthetic chemical from amino acids aspartic acid and phenylalanine with methyl ester. When consumed, the ester breaks down into methanol and may convert into formaldehyde.

I deeply believe we should stay away from any type of synthetic substance and eat more natural.

Many of my patients who drink lots of sodas, suffer from diabetes, overweight, and many neurological problems. My main recommendation is to change their diet. I found it was common among them that they have poor nutrition on top of the excess of drinking sodas because aspartame has addicted properties (acting on dopamine in the central nervous system).

According the U.S. Right to Know (March 2022) many studies have linked aspartame with serious health problems including heart disease, seizures, stroke, obesity, diabetes, cancer and even Alzheimer diseases (due to neurotoxic side effects).

High fructose corn syrup (HFCS) is another sweetener used in many processed foods and different kinds of sodas. It is made from corn starch and known to cause many health problems, including fatty liver, diabetes and obesity. It also could drive inflammation that is associated with heart disease and cancer.

Several research and clinical studies show the danger of high fructose corn syrup to our health.

Based on the National Center for Biotech information (PubMed.gov) an article published by the American Diabetes Association, HFCS causes and increased of triglyceride and insulin resistance, (the main hormone that regulates sugar metabolism), linked to diabetes.

Since the production in the late 1960, HFCS has become the most added sweetener with an exponential increased in consumption.

Research at Princeton University proved the HFCS causes weight gain.

HFCS had been linked to drive inflammation, causing many medical problems, especially heart disease and possible cancer.

One study done at the University of California (UCLA), found that consuming HFCS can affect memory and slow brain function in rats.

How Colors Affect Human Behavior, Chakras and Feng Sui

Color is one of the languages of the soul, and it influences our mood and emotions. Colors have symbolic meanings, which are recognized by our subconscious, but not all colors mean the same to everyone since each culture has different color meanings.

For a long time, color has been studied. This field is called chromology, which is the study of how different colors can affect our mood. When we observe anything that could be perceived as pleasant, it has some type of harmony. Harmony can be defined as a pleasing arrangement of parts, whether it be music, poetry, or COLORS.

In visual experiences, harmony is something that is pleasing to the eye. It engages the viewer and it creates an inner sense of order or balance. When something is not harmonious, it's either boring or chaotic. A visual experience that is so bland can cause the viewer to not be engaged. The brain will not interpret stimulating information well that it cannot organize or understand.

When adding psychology, chromology can help in designing. From rooms to food packaging, it can make us feel many different ways. In the food industry, food is presented to us in different ways and color has a powerful impact.

The classic example is the use of the color green (eco-friendly) on food packaging, which represents a healthy choice and a more natural way of eating.

The color red is used in many restaurants (accent walls or table cloth), and it has been said that hunger becomes more prevalent.

Blue is the opposite of red in regards to stimulation of appetite. Blue causes more relaxation and decreases or suppresses appetite.

Yellow is another appetite stimulator, frequently associated with happiness.

So, we have two stimulating colors in the food industry, red and yellow, which are the colors of the McDonald's logo.

Bright colors usually appear on food to accentuate flavors and are also used on sweets or candies and desserts.

As we are looking at the food package, the brain (eyesight) has only a few seconds to process the product. Do we buy it or not? Consequently, the package needs the best colors and words possible.

Colors strongly influence shoppers in purchase decisions and increased brand awareness.

While the perception of colors is somewhat subjective, color effects do not have universal meaning because it depends on the culture in which we are raised.

Colors are capable of affecting mood and behavior. Colors in the red spectrum are knows as warm colors and include red, orange, and yellow. These warm colors evoke emotions ranging from a feeling of warmth and comfort to a feeling of anger and hostility.

Colors on the blue side of the spectrum are known as cool colors. They include blue, purple, and green. These colors are described as having a calming effect, but, again – that all depends on your culture. While white is associated with purity in the Western world, Eastern cultures often view this color as cold and sterile. Black is the color of mourning in Western countries, while in some East Asian countries, it is white.

It is clear that light is the most important environmental input, after food, in controlling bodily function. Several experiments have shown that different colors affect blood pressure, pulse and respiration rates, as well as brain activity and biorhythms. As a result, colors are now used in the treatment of a variety of diseases.

It is known that the electromagnetic energy of color interacts in some still unknown way with the pituitary and pineal glands and the hypothalamus. These organs regulate the endocrine system, which controls many basic bodily functions and emotional responses, such as aggression.

ENLIGHTNMENT IS A STATE OF BEING

Light affects several types of brain neurotransmitters, allowing chemicals to carry messages from nerve to nerve and from nerve to muscles. Several experiments on rats and small mammals have provided evidence that light striking the retina influences the pineal gland's synthesis of melatonin, a hormone that has been found to help determine the body's output of serotonin (neurotransmitter).

It is well known that serotonin plays an important role in human behavior, since the deficits of serotonin in our brain are linked with depression. This is why antidepressant medications are prescribed, so they can increase the serotonin level in our brain.

In 1942, a Russian scientist named Krakov began to examine color and our autonomic responses. Later, he discovered that red stimulates the sympathetic nervous system (causing it to be exciting), while the color blue stimulates the parasympathetic nervous system (causing relaxation).

Color is all around us. It's everywhere – from the food we eat to when we are looking at our favorite sports team (the color of the jersey). We feel connection.

Color surrounds us physically and psychologically every second of our day, impacting our lives in so many ways, although we are largely unaware of these impacts.

OUR SENSES

Humans have a multitude of senses. Sight (vision), hearing (audition), taste (gustation), smell (olfaction), and touch (somatosensorial) are the five traditionally recognized senses.

There also are non-traditional senses as well, and they are in relation to balance-acceleration, pain, temperature, proprioception and internal senses.

There are perceptions that are not related to a specific sensory organ like time (chronoception), agency or control (subjective awareness), and familiarity (memory).

There also is a sixth sense, an extrasensory perception beyond our five commonly recognized senses.

When we are seeing colors, from the time that it reaches our eyes to the end product, which is the meaning that we give to that specific color, it will have traveled throughout physical and spiritual planes.

The spiritual plane is where the soul resides. Soul is energy. If we could be more aware of this energy, we could be closer to our main essence.

THE MEANING OF THE CHAKRAS

Chakras are centers of energy in our body (which are our psychological, emotional, mental and non-physical areas).

In our soul body, light consists of the seven color energies: red, orange, yellow, green, blue, indigo and violet. Each color is connected to various areas of our body and will affect our emotions, physical being and mental state differently. By learning how each color influences us, we can effectively use color to help us at different levels.

As we know, our mind interacts with our body, and the harmony of both lead us to a healthy state of being.

Because these vital energy centers cannot be detected by modern medical means, the Western traditional medicine may not support the existence of chakras.

There are seven main centers (chakras) of the body and each center is represented by a different color, from the violet which is the crown, to the red which is the base in our pelvic area.

To be healthy, we need a balance between body, mind and spirit, and I believe that colors have a profound effect on us on all three levels.

When the seven chakras are aligned, there is good energy flow creating harmony and health.

When this center of energy is blocked or depleted, then our body cannot function properly and this, in turn, can lead to a variety of problems on any level.

To understand how it works, let's say we have a disruption at the throat chakra (blue), which relates to the spiritual aspect of self-expression (communication), the energy in this area will not be free flowing. By using more blue, it will help us with this kind of problem. Blue is great for relaxation, ideal for sleep problems and even for hyper-active children. Blue connects us to holistic thoughts and gives us wisdom and clarity, enhancing communication and speech.

I believe the main causes of blocking these chakras or not allowing this natural energy flow are high levels of stress, anxiety or depression.

Every color has a meaning and different vibrations of energy that will affect us in a variety of ways.

All the chakras can be unblocked by being close to nature, with positive affirmations, through meditation or by using specific crystals or stones.

Chakras

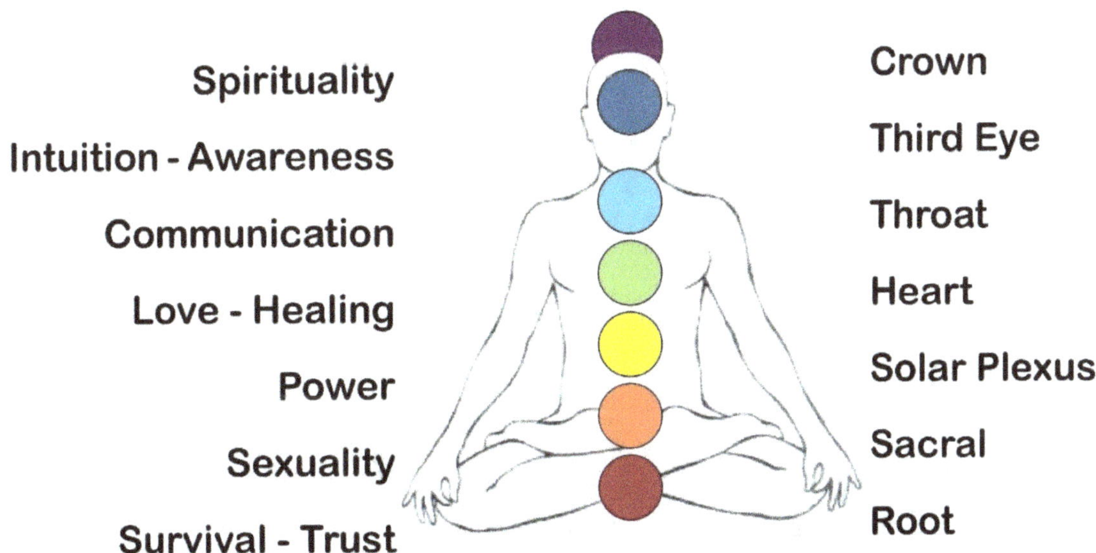

THE NATURAL MEANING AND MEDICAL ILLNESSES RELATED TO EACH CHAKRA, AND HOW TO UNBLOCK IT

Crown Chakra

THE COLOR FOR THIS CHAKRA IS VIOLET (combination of RED and BLUE).

This color represents self-awareness, talent, creativity and consciousness. It is a calming color and great for meditation.

The use of this color can help us if we suffer from headaches, tremors, depression, memory problems or seizures.

To unblock: Be at peace with yourself, pray to be connected with the supreme energy of the universe.

Affirmation: I am infinite and eternal energy.

Crystals: In the colors of violet or clear like clear quartz, diamond, selenite or amethyst.

Third Eye or Brow Chakra

THE COLOR OF THIS CHAKRA IS INDIGO (WHICH IS A DARK BLUE with a dash of violet).

This color represents intuition, mysticism, understanding and awareness.

The use of this color helps to open intuition, has a calming effect and is related to high mind and divine knowledge.

When this chakra is blocked, it could manifest trouble making choices or decisions or feeling we do not have any purpose in life.

The use of this color can help for insomnia, headaches and seizures.

To unblock: Be intuitive and honest with yourself, trust your decision.

Affirmation: I am connected with the wisdom of the universe and trust my intuition.

Crystals: In the purple or dark colors like amethyst, black obsidian and purple fluorite.

Throat Chakra

THE COLOR OF THIS CHAKRA IS BLUE (A PRIMARY COLOR).

Blue is the color associated with heaven, with a meaning of pure, soothing, calming and healing energy.

The throat chakra is responsible for communication, self-expression and truth.

A block on this chakra could be related to sore throat, thyroid disease, the inability to express feelings (speech related problems) or mouth-teeth problems.

Wearing blue colored clothing and singing or expressing ourselves can help to balance this chakra.

To unblock: Need positive affirmations, be faithful to yourself, tell the truth.

Affirmation: I always speak the truth easily.

Crystals: In the blue tones like turquoise, aquamarine or lapis lazuri.

Heart Chakra

THE COLOR OF THIS CHAKRA IS GREEN (combination of yellow and blue).

Green is the energy of love and compassion, at the very center of our being, the heart center. It is where we connect with something greater and deeper. Green is the color of growth, nature   and balance, and brings peace and harmony to our life.

If this chakra is blocked, we experience emotional instability in our relationship and are unable to express unconditional love, compassion or forgiveness.

Related problems if this chakra is blocked could be heart disease, blood

BEING QUICK IS NOT ALWAYS FASTER

pressure issues, fatigue or pulmonary illness.

To unblock: love yourself, be in a stable relationship, hug your pets (cats or dogs), stay close to nature.

Affirmation: My heart is open with unconditional love, giving and receiving easily.

Crystals: In the green-pink colors like green calcite, rhodonite, rose quartz or jade.

Solar Chakra

THE COLOR OF THIS CHAKRA IS YELLOW (primary color).

The main function of this chakra is to stimulate your mental activity, and to enhance clear intentions and desires of our personal goals.

It is associated with the expression of will and strength of our ideas.

This chakra gives us clarity of judgment, helping us to stay alert, confident, gives wisdom and boosts self-esteem.

When this chakra is aligned, it allows us to have a healthy ego and self-esteem. When it is not aligned, the energy flow is blocked. It could result in low self-esteem, lots of fears, digestive problems, peptic ulcers, abdominal cramps and tiredness.

To unblock: deep breathing, meditation, know you have unlimited potential.

Affirmation: I can do anything I want because I am powerful and worthy.

Crystals: In the yellow colors like lemon quartz, yellow jasper or citrine.

Sacral Chakra

THE COLOR OF THIS CHAKRA IS ORANGE (combination of red and yellow)

This chakra is located in the lower abdomen, and is connected with the reproductive system. It is associated with our emotional responses, creativity, sexuality, sensual pleasure, intuition and emotional intelligence.

Dysfunction or blockage of this chakra is associated with male and female reproductive problems (testicular, prostate, ovaries, pre-menstrual syndrome, miscarriages and sexual dysfunctions).

An opened and balanced sacral chakra may allow us to experience intimacy freely.

To unblock: embrace your sexuality and pleasure, remove guilt, unleash creativity.

Affirmation: I feel grateful and enjoy the pleasure of my body and my life.

Crystals: In the orange colors like amber, orange calcite or tiger eye.

Root or Base Chakra

THE COLOR OF THIS CHAKRA IS RED (PRIMARY COLOR).

The root chakra is located at the base of the spine, and is the first chakra and the root of the entire chakra system. It is associated with feeling grounded, safe, vital and self-confident. It represents the energy at the base of the spine and may be the point where the energy enters the body (according to some yoga teachers).

The stronger our root chakra is, the better chance of survival we have.

Imbalance of the root chakra can be related to behavior of addiction, eating disorders, anxiety, fears, low back pain and bladder or prostate problems.

To unblock: walking barefoot on the ground or beach sand.

Affirmation: I am grounded and nourished by this earth.

Crystals: in the red-black colors like black onyx, hematite, red jasper or red calcite.

It has been said that the seven chakras have to do with the seven-year cycles of our life.

Starting with the Root Chakra, the first seven years of our life is about survival and dependent from our parents for nourishment.

The Sacral Chakra (7 to 14 years) is when we go into puberty and sexual development.

The Solar Chakra (14 to 21 years) is when we develop a sense of purpose and wisdom.

The Heart Chakra (21 to 28 years) is about emotions and relationships or when considering marriage.

The Throat Chakra (28 to 35 years) is when we are beginning our own careers and communication becomes crucial.

The Third Eye **and the** Crown chakras (late 30s and 40s) we are becoming self-aware and more spiritual.

COLORS IN THE ENVIRONMENT

All colors we use will depend on its tone (color plus gray), its tint (color plus white), or its shades (color plus black) for a psychological meaning.

Also, all colors have intensity(brightness or dullness).

The hue is the name of the specific color (blue, green, red, etc.).

Remember, colors are not universal since they have different meanings, depending on the culture we live in or grew up in.

The two colors that have no hues are black and white.

BLACK: GIVES US REFLECTION AND INNER SEARCHING.

WHITE: CONTAINS ALL THE COLORS, EMPHASIZES PURITY AND ILLUMINATES OUR THOUGHTS, GIVING US CLARITY.

I believe having the right color in our home is a very important way to start having a positive environment. Knowing the meaning and importance of each color could help us to live in a more positive and healthy way.

VIOLET/PURPLE (blue and red)

Historically, it is a color associated with wealth, royalty and power. In accent walls, it gives a feeling of sophistication and glamor. It is great for churches, entryways of clinics or hospitals, and festival areas. In bedrooms, it is better to use lighter shades or tones, like lavender.

The color purple is the color of intuition and perception and is helpful in opening the Third Eye (located on the forehead between the eyebrows). It is said that it is the central point of intuition and inner wisdom. It promotes deep concentration during times of introspection and meditation, helping you to achieve deeper levels of consciousness.

INDIGO (dark blue)

It is good for quiet places, like the bedroom or treatment rooms. It can be used in similar rooms where blue was used. Avoid using blue in the kitchen, it can suppress the appetite.

BLUE

It can be used in almost any room, like the bedroom or spa. It should not be used in the area we exercise or play, due to the calming and relaxation impact. Because blue also stimulates creativity and concentration, it is great for offices and scholastic environments.

It is great for the bedroom when used in darker shades, due to the calming effect, which allows us to rest and sleep peacefully. Due to this effect on people, it is known to lower blood pressure and calm the cardiovascular system.

If you are looking to stimulate your appetite and make food the main topic for socialization, it is recommended to avoid blue in the dining area, since it can suppress the appetite (blue color is rare in natural food, animal or plant types of food).

GREEN

It is a very universal color and can be used in most areas, depending on its shade. It is associated with nature, vegetation and also wealth.

In the bedroom, it is softer to the eyes and helps to relax. In the bathroom, using a blue-leaning shade of green gives you a relaxing and spa-like

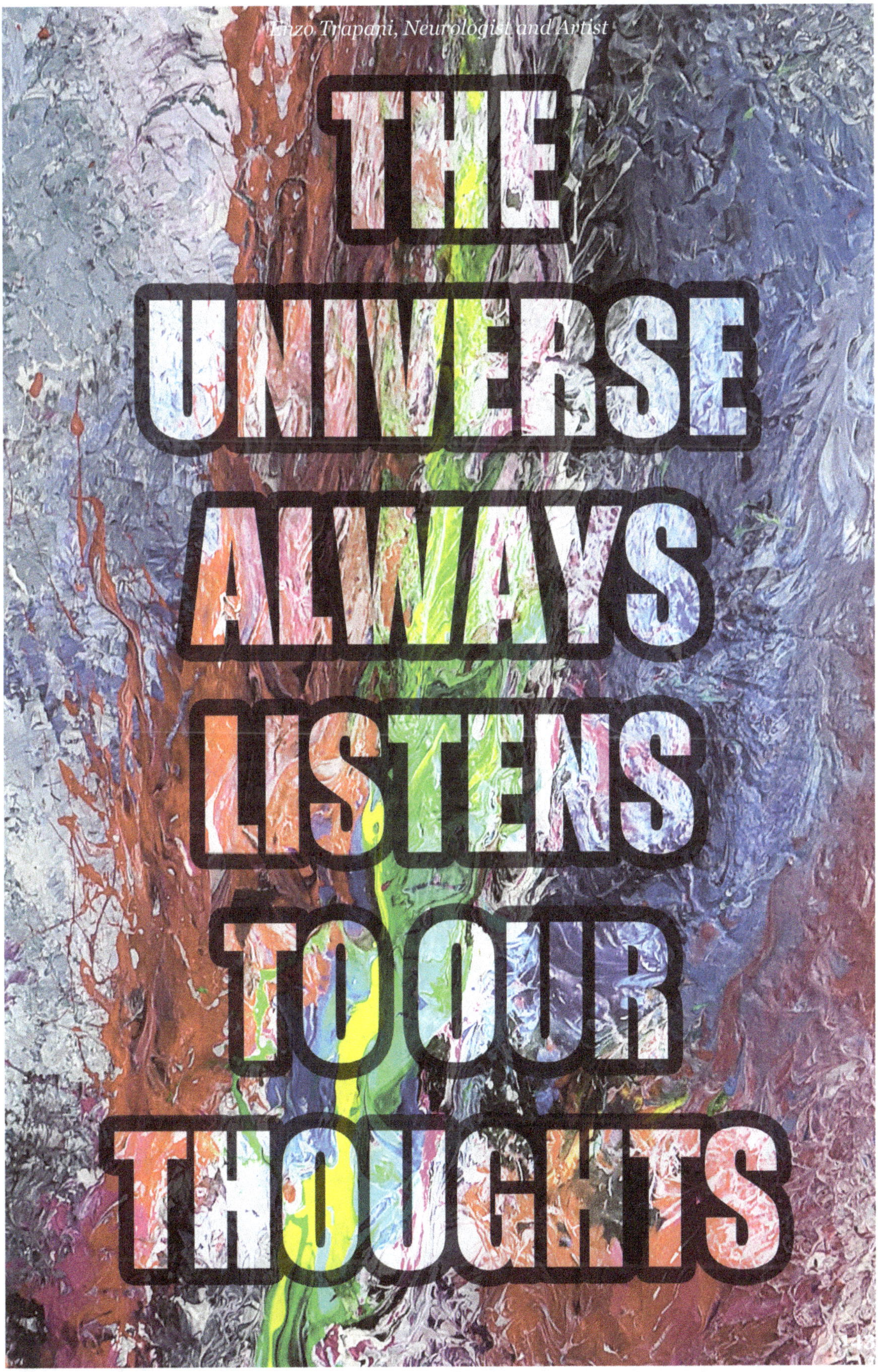

THE UNIVERSE ALWAYS LISTENS TO OUR THOUGHTS

feeling. In the living or dining area, it helps you to unwind, socialize and inter-act. In the office, it may help with concentration. Green   also is often associ-ated with feelings of calmness and is easy on the eyes.

Many home decorators will tell you that green reminds us of nature or an outdoor feeling, therefore we like creating this feeling while sitting comfortably in our living room.

Science of People research lab recommends painting your office green (or blue), because those colors increase efficiency and mood. It is a restful color for our eyes and also has some calming qualities, depending on the hues.

It is my favorite color in the living room.

YELLOW

This color represents optimism, enlightenment and happiness. It can be used to warm up the room on long winter days (representing sunlight). It is great for an activity room, but not for the bedroom since it may interfere with sleep. In small spaces, like a narrow corridor, yellow can help to visually expand the area.

It is a clean color and is friendly in the bathroom. On an accent wall with white, it could compliment very well in lighter shades. It increases mental activ-ity and activates the memory.

Using yellow in a classroom may encourage children to be creative and it creates a positive feeling.

Yellow and light green are my favorite colors for the kitchen.

ORANGE

It is a bright, energetic, vibrant, playful and a fun color. Orange may stim-ulate appetite and is great for accent walls in restaurants. It may enhance social interaction.

This color is great in creative areas. If you like a Mediterranean flavor, it is better used in lighter or different terracotta shades.

RED

Red brings warmth, energy and stimulation. Therefore, it is good for energy and for fighting fatigue and poor concentration. Red energizes the heart and blood circulation, increasing sexual desire and increasing body temperature.

The color red represents many things, including vitality, courage, self-confidence, passion, sexuality, joy, anger, love   and happiness. In China, it means socialism-communism (after the twentieth century).

It is a very vibrant and powerful color, never boring. In any room, it enhances passion and energy. In a bedroom, it should be used in a lighter shade, since an intense red could increase the heart rate and/or blood pressure.

Red also can be used in your home to set the mood. For example, you may want to consider red for your living room, as it can boost social energy. It is a very popular color in restaurants and can be used in a dining area as it increases appetite and socialization.

Red is good for any activity area. It's great for accent walls since it stimulates excitement and creates a strong impression.

BLACK

This color is associated with power, prestige, sophistication and elegance. It almost always compliments other colors. However, note that it can make the area appear smaller unless used on accent walls.

Black is a great color for furniture or entry doors (it creates a protective and solid energy).

Black is the most mysterious of all colors, and is the color of the void and sophistication. It may enhance the good energy in your home through feng shui.

BROWN

Brown represents nature and earth, and is warm and inviting. It is associ-

WE ARE WHAT WE THINK

ated with health and outdoor activities. This color is great for socializing areas.

PINK

It inspires creativity and balance, and is recommended for the bedroom and working space. Pink is often a color that is tied to femininity, but it also has a calming effect on people. Pink is essentially a light red and may be associated with love and romance.

The color pink represents compassion, nurture and love. It relates to unconditional love and understanding, and the giving and receiving of nurturing.

In the Western society, pink is applied to girl s' rooms. However, in France, the color pink is seen more in male fashion.

I always wondered when and why pink became a female symbol. According to my research, it was before the 1900 s that blue and pink were the appropriate colors for babies and children, but it was not until the 1980 s that pink became a strong symbol of femininity.

This color is associated with purity, innocence and serenity. It always makes any room feel larger. The positive aspect could be the meaning of simplicity, freshness and cleanliness. The negative aspect could be coldness, isolation or sterility. It's great for accent areas like windows or door frames.

Since we are mentioning how color can influence human behavior, it is important to see how animals can communicate through colors.

Animals can use colors to camouflage or attract attention.

One color that is fascinating is iridescence, the hue of this color depends on the position of the viewer and the direction of light, and will keep changing depending on the angle of the observer.

The iridescent color is used by the butterfly, hummingbird or seen on peacock feathers. Hummingbirds' throats appear bright pink for female attraction. Other animals use bright colors to warn other animals that they are poisonous.

A fascinating event in nature is how chameleons can change colors. It is known that many factors can cause this incredible phenomenon. One theory is that temperatures around them is the cause. When the chameleon is cold, its skin becomes darker, knowing that dark colors absorb light. They use their skin color like a thermostat. When they are hot, they turn into lighter shades to absorb less light since it is known that white colors reflect light. Another possible reason that chameleons change colors is based on their mood.

FENG SHUI

Feng Sui (ancient Chinese art of space arrangement) is a philosophy of arranging and positioning furniture and architecture design in your home. The goal is to create a balance of energy and harmony in your house.

In the Asian culture, it is called the Tao, meaning, the way. In other words, it is to balance the energy in one place for better harmony. It teaches us what and where to place things, to use the right colors, materials and shapes for the purpose of a better environment. Feng shui uses universal principles and laws of nature for better energy in your house.

An example is the front door of the house, called the "mouth of chi," which helps to bring good energy into your house. It is important to keep it clean and well-lit. Each specific color has its own representation, like red for energy and wealth, blue for relaxation, or green to bring growth.

Feng shui uses five elements to balance the energy in your house. They are water, fire, earth, metal and wood. These five elements come from Taoism (700 BC), which describes how these elements interact and resonate with each other.

Not only does the element add a material subject to the environment, but it enhances the energy that is associated with this subject. Simply, it is adding the energy that we are lacking or missing in us.

Water is always associated with cleansing, movement and purification.

The way Feng Sui brings this element into the house is by adding blues, objects with curves or simply showing images of water.

Fire is a powerful element and is related to action, passion, emotional expression and strong energy. A simple way to show fire is to add more red, pink or orange in the room.

Metal means wealth, clarity and helps us to focus. Metal has some cold, rigid and rational features. To activate the metal quality though color, you should add pastel, white or gray. Use of chairs and other metallic finishes or objects like sculptures can be utilized to enhance metal.

Earth is associated with stability, keeping us grounded and feeling secure. Earth tones are always a form of brown. Design ideas can be done using ceramics or terra cotta pots with soft colors on the fabrics. We may need more earth elements if we are anxious or ungrounded.

Wood is a symbol of new life, growth, healing and health. Adding wood into the house can be done with real plants (plastic plants have dead energy), wood furniture or wood floors. The main color that represents wood is green.

Every canvas I work on, I transfer my energy and feelings into the colors that I use, which I hope will be portrayed to the person looking at my art.

We are attracted to the color we are missing in us. It is like when we are hungry, we eat to become satisfied. It is the same with colors. If we are missing a color in ourselves, then we crave more of that specific color.

That is the reason I introduced the "PILL ON THE WALL" to have a piece of what we love on the wall.

I believe I am mixing colors based on my instinct and less on my intellect.

A painting on the wall will be the representation of a piece of emotion, awareness of the environment we live in and the repercussions in our health and it is my intention to reach people's feelings through colors and forms.

WE ARE ALL CONNECTED

The Visual Pathway

The human eye is the most important organ that allows us to see light. As I tell many of my patients, the eyes are a piece of the brain sticking out. First of all, we need to know that the iris regulates the amount of light entering into the eye and the pupils are the circular openings in the center of the iris.

The cornea is a transparent membrane in front of the eye that reflects the light entering the eyes and the lens is a transparent structure behind the pupils.

Stimulation of the pupils will cause the pupils to dilate, and the system that controls the pupil's size is called the autonomic system.

The autonomic system consists of the sympathetic and parasympathetic systems. When the sympathetic system is activated, which could be triggered by the use of cocaine or a natural emotional response like attraction for something or fear, then the pupil will dilate (mydriasis).

The muscle that controls the pupil is called the iris.

If the other system is stimulated (the parasympathetic system), the pupils constrict (miosis). The normal eye response to light is to constrict the pupils (monitoring the amount of light entering into the brain), but drugs like opioids could also constrict the pupils.

The retina is a thin layer of tissue that lines the back of the eye, projected into the optic nerves. What the retina does is convert the LIGHT into neural signals, sending messages to the brain for visual recognition.

In the retina, the eye cell's neurons are the cones and rods. The cones are concentrated in the macula (center of the retina) and the rods are concentrated at the outer edge of the retina. Rods work at very low levels of light, predominantly for night vision. Cones are responsible for color vision and function best in the bright light during day time. These photoreceptors (cones and rods) convert photons (particles of light) into chemical and electrical stimuli that can be processed by the visual center in the brain.

It is interesting to know that light energy can be transformed into chemical energy by the cells in the retina. It is similar to PHOTOSYNTHESIS, where light energy also becomes chemical energy by PLANTS, and that is how the plant gets its own food. Sunlight energy is converted into chemical energy. Chlorophyll (the green pigment) absorbs the light using energy to convert water and carbon dioxide into glucose. During this process, oxygen is released into the atmosphere. This is the reason it is important to keep trees on this planet.

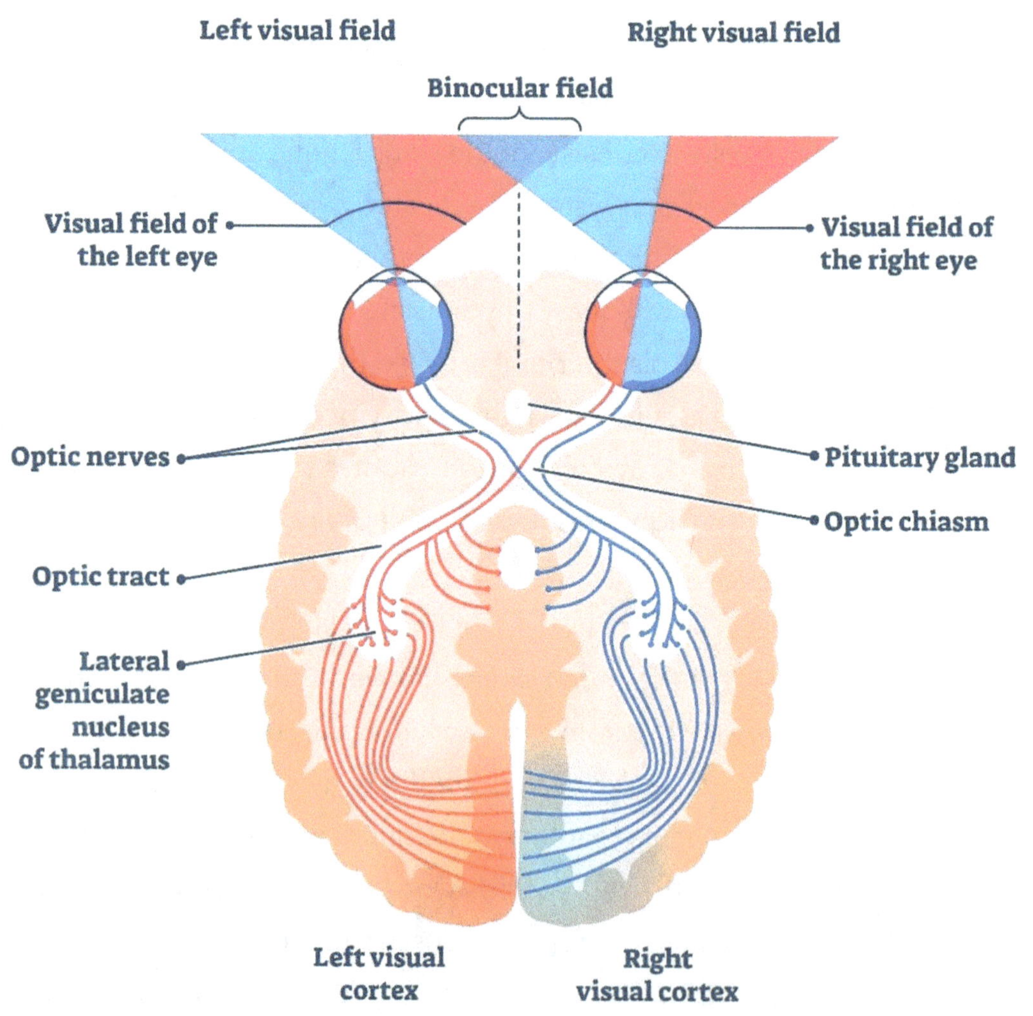

Monochrome vision (which occurs in the rod cells) and color vision (which occurs in the cone cells) are the first steps where light is transformed into the chemical component that will travel through the central nervous system.

The eyes only have one type of ROD cell, but have three different types of CONE cells. The difference between the three types of cone cells, as we shall see, allows us to distinguish colors.

Of the three types of cones, the "green" and "red" cones are mostly packed into the fovea centralis (in the macula, center of the retina).

When light strikes a cone, it interacts with a visual pigment, which consists of a protein called opsin and a small molecule called a chromophore, which in humans is a derivative of VITAMIN A. Three different kinds of opsins respond to short, medium and long wavelengths of light.

Photoreceptor cell

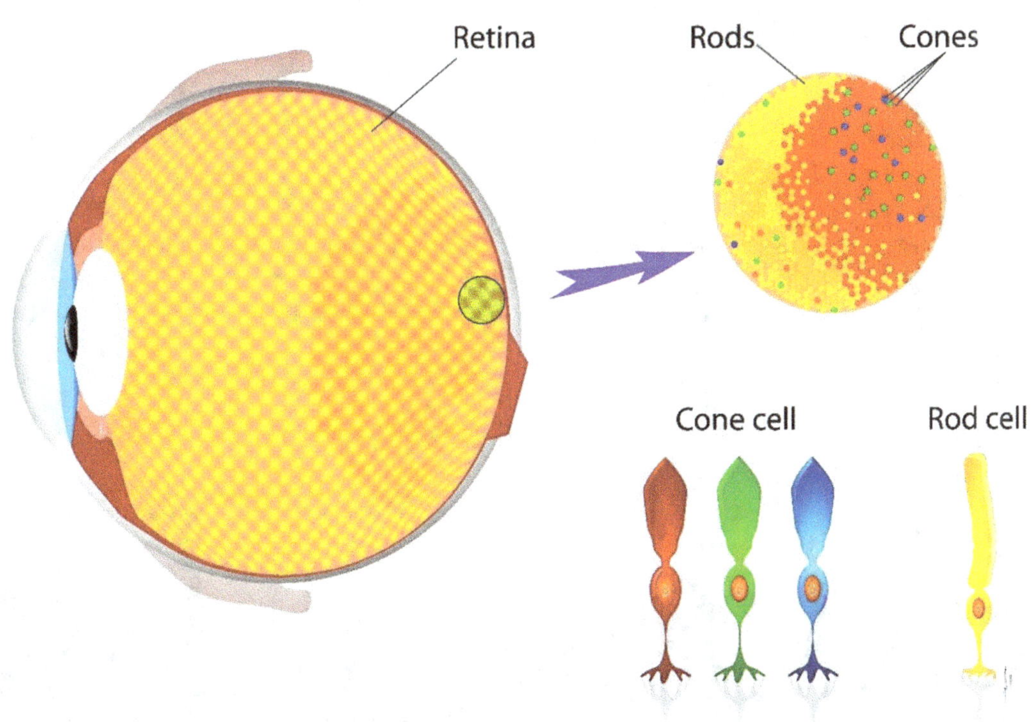

WHEN TREES LOSE THEIR LEAVES, IT MAKES ROOM FOR OTHERS TO GROW

Light Entering the Eye

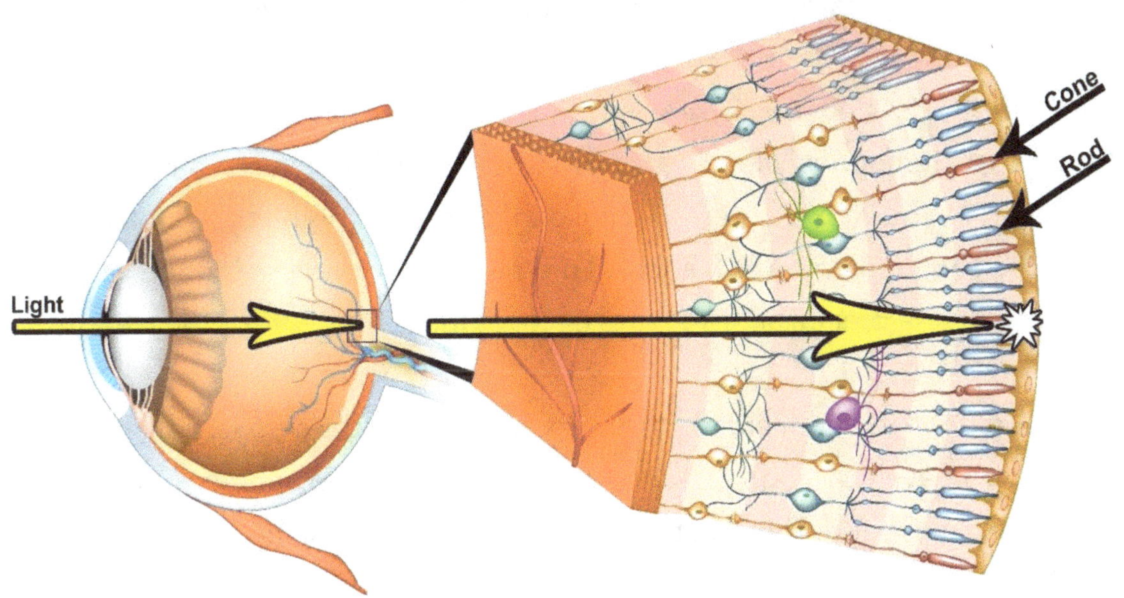

For a person to see an object in color, at least two kinds of cones must be triggered, and the observation of color is based on the relative level of excitation of the different cones.

The information received by the cells in the retina (from the cones and rods) will send the signal to the eye nerve (called the optic nerve).

The optic nerve emerges from the optic disc in the retina, sending the signal to the visual center of the brain (the optic nerve is an extension of the retina).

During this pathway, from the retina to the end of the visual center in the brain (the occipital lobe), the light signal information interacts through many stations before reaching its final destination (brain nucleus, temporal-parietal lobes, association cortex and the limbic system).

The temporal lobe governs recognition and memory, the parietal lobes are responsible for motion and spatial analysis, while the limbic system relates to emotions. The association areas of the brain (areas of the brain that connect with each other) interact with other areas including auditory, motor, visual and sensory centers.

When we look at one specific color, it will cause many other responses including sensory, emotional or the remembering of a specific memory. Each center of the brain talks to other centers of the brain; they always talk to each other.

Another system that is very important to mention is the limbic system (house of the emotional life). Ever since I was in medical school, I have been fascinated by the limbic system, because that structure of the brain houses emotions and memories (new and old memories). This system is not a well-defined area in the brain. This also plays a role in the smell center, motivation and behavior.

From the moment light enters into our visual pathway, a large amount of information travels through the brain, triggering emotions, memories and photographing our world. This creates a reality and gives meaning to everything we observe.

LOVE IS LIGHT WITHOUT OPPOSITION

How Vision Changes as We Age

As our physical strength decreases with age, our vision also declines in performance. It is considered normal to lose focus, and it can become a challenge to distinguish colors such as blue from black or we may need more light to see well. We find ourselves squinting a little more to read emails on our phone.

As the light enters into the eye, the first point of entry is the cornea and the cornea is lubricated by tears to maintain a smooth surface and precise image. Any abnormal production of tears will lead to a breakdown of the corneal surface (Dry eyes syndrome), leading to degradation of images. It is treated with artificial tear drops. The risk for dry eyes increases in women after menopause.

One of the most common eye problems we encounter, especially past the milestone age of 40, is called PRESBYOPIA (from the Greek words presbus meaning old man, and opia meaning eye). Presbyopia is the inability to focus on nearby objects, causing us to place objects further away to read. It is the lack of ability to focus due to the hardening of the lens inside our eye (the lens inside the eye becomes less flexible). The simple correction of presbyopia is the use of reading or bifocal glasses (the top part of the glasses corrects for distance vision and the lower section corrects for closer vision).

The other most common problem is cataracts. After age 65, our eyes start to become cloudy and we start to see with blurred vision. Light has more glare; the sun becomes too bright and we also start losing the brightness of colors. The treatment for cataracts is removing the clouded lens and replacing it with a clear artificial lens. It will remain a permanent part of your eye.

Another important change in our vision is that our pupils become smaller. That is because the muscles that control our pupil size and reaction to light are losing strength. As a result, the pupils react more sluggish to light and dilate more slowly in the dark.

Normal pupil size in adults is 2- 4 mm in diameter in bright light and 4-8 mm at dark. In our 60s, we need three times more light than those in their 20 s (the brain is getting less light).

Another physical change in our eyes is the inability to move our eyes as before and we start to lose strength in the eye muscles.

Our eyes move in different directions by complex muscle coordination. One of the most common physical findings I encounter in my practice is that people start losing the "up gaze," resulting in the inability to look up. The reason this occurs is because our body starts curving down as we age, so we start looking down more often. We should try to keep our posture straight, which will keep our head up.

We also start losing our peripheral vision and our visual field becomes smaller (especially after the age of 70). We could lose approximately 20 degrees of visibility (this is important to determine especially when driving a car).

Decreased color vision also is very common because the cells (photoreceptors) that are responsible for our normal color vision in the retina declines, colors become less bright and the color contrasts are less noticeable. For example, the color blue becomes more faded and/or washed out.

The substance between the eye lens and the retina is a gel-like material called vitreous. This substance can detach from the retina causing floaters, or spots, and sometimes it's like flashes of light (vitreous detachment). It is a harmless condition, but it is always important to check with the doctor since seeing a floater or flashes could be a sign of retinal detachment (a more serious condition).

To maintain a normal, healthy vision, it is very important to have a healthy diet and wise lifestyle choices.

Not only do our eyes change as we age, but the way we process colors change as well. Some of these ways are visual processing speeds, dark adaptation, and seeing under low illumination or spatial contrast adaptation. All of these mechanisms can be affected.

YOUR
MIND IS
THE BIGGEST
CANVAS FOR
CREATION

It is not clear what all of the changes are that occur in the brain as we age, but it is known that there are many changes occurring at the molecular, vasculature and cellular level.

In my experience, I have many elderly patients and they have brain atrophy (brain volume loss) on the brain MRI, predominantly in the frontal-temporal area – the area that is important in cognition, memory and behavior.

To process colors, not only do we need an intact visual pathway, but we also require areas that are connected to the visual pathway. Brain association areas are connected to the visual pathways, which was explained in the chapter, The Visual Pathway, with other centers where emotions or memories reside.

Many other factors play roles in having a healthy eyesight and brain: genetics, hormones, neurochemicals, environment and nutrition. We can prevent cardiovascular diseases by controlling high blood pressure, avoiding smoking and high alcohol consumption, correcting cholesterol levels, and improving physical activities. Controlling these risk factors will lead us to healthy eyes and a healthy mind.

Medical Conditions Affecting Our Vision

There are many types of medical conditions that affect our visual system. Many are treatable while others, unfortunately, have no cure. We can help in our eye health by living a healthy lifestyle and visiting an eye professional regularly.

Following are the most common medical conditions affecting our vision.

Myopia (nearsighted)

Myopia is a very common condition and is a refractive error, meaning the eye is unable to refract the light correctly. It is because the eyeball is too long and the light cannot focus correctly. The images focus in front of the retina with this condition. To have a clear image, the object that we are looking at, the light of the object has to focus in the retina. People can see close objects clearly, but objects farther away are blurred. Myopia affects more than 20 percent of the population and can be easily corrected with eyeglasses, contact lenses or surgery.

Hyperopia (farsighted)

Hyperopia is the opposite of myopia and the focus of light is behind the retina. It is a common visual condition where we can see distant objects clearly, but objects nearby may be blurry. It usually tends to run in families and can be easily corrected with eyeglasses or contact lenses.

Color blindness

Color blindness or more accurately, color vision deficiency, is an inherited condition that affects males more frequently than females. According to Prevent Blindness America, about 8 percent of males and less than 1 percent of females have color vision problems. Red-green color deficiency is the most common form of color blindness.

Because the problem of color blindness is based at the cells of the retina (photoreceptors) and at the optic nerve or at the visual center, the cure for this condition is limited.

Cataracts

Cataracts are a very common condition mainly affecting people in the later stages of life. It is a cloudiness of the normal lens inside the eyes. People start having cloudy, blurred or foggy vision, and it becomes difficult to read or drive (especially at night). The final treatment for this condition is surgical correction by replacing the cloudy lens with a clear artificial lens.

Glaucoma

Glaucoma is a disease of the eyes caused by abnormal high pressure inside the eyes, causing damage to the optic nerve. It is one of the leading causes of blindness for people older than 60. The real cause of glaucoma is unknown, but a potential inflammatory factor, as well as genetic and retinal blood flow abnormalities, may contribute to the role in glaucoma.

We may have it without any warning signs, so regular checkups with the eye doctor to measure the eye pressure is important.

When there is an increased intraocular pressure, the night vision becomes poor and we start to see blind spots or start losing our eye sight. We may experience patchy blind spots in one or both eyes, and experience tunnel vision in more advanced stages. In acute presentation of glaucoma, we could have headaches, eye pain or eye redness.

The holistic or natural remedy for glaucoma should start with a healthy lifestyle, including regular exercise, a healthy diet and consuming appropriate vitamins.

Eliminating inflammatory food (processed foods, food high in sugar) and adding more antioxidants is extremely important, considering that glaucoma could be due to inflammation or oxidative stress in our body.

Adding dark, leafy greens (broccoli, kale and spinach), berries (blueberries, blackberries), magnesium, vitamin C, Ginkgo Biloba, omega-3 fatty acids (found in fish oil) is an excellent start.

Acupuncture may have some benefits to treating glaucoma.

I deeply believe in medical cannabis to aid in reducing intraocular pressure. I do recommend not to vape, but to use tincture oil.

Some studies showed that THC (tetrahydrocannabinol), which is a type of marijuana, helps to treat glaucoma.

Using daily eyedrops or taking regular oral medication is the standard treatment for glaucoma.

When glaucoma cannot be controlled with daily medications, surgery with laser or other surgical procedure is implemented.

Macular degeneration

Macula is the area in the center of the retina layer, where the light is focused and sends pictures to the visual center of the brain. The exact cause of this condition is unknown, but factors that influence this deterioration include advanced age, smoking, high blood pressure, family history, obesity and high cholesterol levels.

The person begins to lose the center of the vision, the vision can become blurred and colors begin to look faded, possibly leading to blindness.

Nutrition is crucial in the treatment of this condition, with high levels of antioxidants to support the cells in the macula. The other treatment is laser therapy to destroy the abnormal blood vessels.

Retinal detachment

Retinal detachment occurs when the retina pulls away from the back of the eye, losing blood supply. The cells will stop getting oxygen and nourishment, causing the retinal cells to die.

The retina has all the cells to send the light signal information into the brain. Without the retina, we start losing vision, begin to see floaters, and experience sensations of shade or curtains across the visual field.

Some risk factors play a role in having retinal detachment and that includes aging (more frequent in people older than 50), diabetes mellitus, extreme myopia, previous eye injury and family history of the same condition.

The treatment for retinal detachment includes proper nutrition (nutrition alone will not treat this condition, but helps to keep the retina healthy). This includes foods rich in vitamin C (citrus, peaches), A (carrots, beef liver, pumpkin), E (hazelnut and almond), and foods rich in omega 3-fatty acid (salmon).

For a retinal tear, laser therapy or a freezing (cryopexy) technique may be required.

For a full retinal detachment, injecting a bubble of air or gas into the eye may help to push the retina into the right place.

Optic neuritis

Optic neuritis is an inflammation of the optic nerve, the nerve responsible for sending the information to the brain to process all our vision. The presentation is pain or flashing lights on eye movement or visual loss.

One of the most common causes is multiple sclerosis, a disease in which our autoimmune system attacks the sheath covering the nerve fibers in the brain. Infections like syphilis, Lyme's disease or a virus can affect the optic nerve.

Other diseases like Sarcoidosis or lupus may cause optic neuritis.

Toxins like methanol found in solvents, antifreeze or in paints could affect the optic nerve. The treatment will depend on the cause of this condition.

Migraine headaches

Migraine headaches can affect our vision and can cause temporal visual loss, shades, and/or seeing spots, zigzag lines or halos in the visual field.

Migraines are the third most prevalent illness in the world, and in the USA, almost one in four may suffer from some type of migraine, with a high prevalence in women.

Many factors play a role in the cause of migraines. Genetic tendency (family history) is an important factor, but main triggers could be alcohol, food, weather changes (barometric temperature), stress and anxiety, lack of sleep or hormonal changes.

The main treatment is prevention and treating of the acute attack. Proper nutrition and regular exercise help to prevent migraine headaches.

Supplements for migraine prevention include vitamin B (B2 or riboflavin), Magnesium, vitamin D and Coenzyme Q10 (is a substance that help to generate energy and protect the cells from oxidative damage).

There is one type of headache that requires special attention. It is not a migraine type and is called Idiopathic Intracranial Hypertension (IIH), also called pseudotumor cerebri. This headache affects mainly obese women of childbearing age and the most important manifestation is that the optic nerve starts to swell, leading to partial or total visual loss.

The cause is unknown, but occurs due to increased intracranial pressure. The reason that I mention this condition is because weight loss could improve this condition, and also with the help of medication like diuretics. When all conservative treatment has failed, eye surgery is needed (optic nerve sheath fenestration) to preserve the vision.

Temporal arteritis

Temporal arteritis is an inflammation of the artery that supplies blood to the optic nerve and could lead to blindness. The most common complaint is headache, visual loss, generalized pain or low-grade fever, especially in people older than 60. The diagnosis of this condition can be done with blood testing called temporal artery biopsy.

The treatment for this condition is steroids. As the optic nerve gets deeper into the brain, it forms the Optic Chiasm (where the optic nerves cross).

HONESTY IS LIBERATION

This structure can be compressed by tumors in the pituitary gland, which controls other hormone glands, like thyroid and adrenal.As a tumor grows, it can affect our vision.

Stroke

Stroke is the third leading cause of death in the United States of America and is a leading cause of long-term disability.

There are two types of strokes. One is called ischemic (lack of blood due to a plaque inside the blood vessel) and the other one is called hemorrhagic (brain bleed). The most common one is the ischemic type. People with hypertension, chronic smoking and diabetes are more prone to have this type of stroke.

Stroke in the brain can lead to visual changes including blindness, especially if the stroke affects the temporal, parietal or occipital lobes. Consequently, it affects the color perception and interpretation. I have always been fascinated by the lesion in the brain that causes change in perception, especially colors.

Cortical blindness is usually due to lesions of the primary visual cerebral cortex from a stroke and patients will be totally blind.

A lesion in the posterior occipital and or temporal lobe could lead to another condition and is called AGNOSIAS.

Visual agnosia is the inability to recognize familiar objects. One can see, but they cannot recognize a spouse or other relative and it may happen after a stroke or dementia.

Alzheimer's disease

The visual center (occipital lobe) in the brain is interconnected with association areas, which are centers where higher processing information is located in the temporal, parietal and frontal lobes. It is where the auditory, motor, sensory and memory areas interconnect with the limbic system. This limbic system is one of the most important centers and is responsible for processing our emotions, and is the key center for memory (short and long term).

These areas (association center) govern visual recognition and memory, and are responsible for motion and spatial analysis. As we see, everything in the brain is interconnected. When we see something, it can trigger a recall with an emotional response.

These association areas are very susceptible to be affected in people with Alzheimer's because the "amyloid plaques and neurofibrillary tangles" (two pathological abnormalities commonly seen in Alzheimer diseases) usually are concentrated in these areas of the brain. These lesions are in the memory center, and are the reason that the main complaint of Alzheimer's is memory loss. The most common type of dementia in the United States of America is Alzheimer's and more than 3 million cases are reported. Worldwide at least more than 40 million people are living with dementia.

To clarify, dementia is a syndrome (group of signs and symptoms) and can be caused by many medical conditions including stroke (vascular dementia), chronic alcohol abuse, HIV, Parkinson's diseases, traumatic brain injury, malnutrition, thyroid disease and heavy metal poison, but the most common type of dementia in the United States is Alzheimer's disease   .

The main diagnosis for Alzheimer's is based on clinical impression, including the history obtained by the patient or from the family.

People with Alzheimer's disease have significant visual problems, such as recognizing familiar faces or color cues, but the most common complaint is short term memory. When it is advanced, the long-term memory is affected. Alzheimer patients commonly have a condition, called agnosias, which is the inability to process sensory information. Patients lose the ability to recognize familiar objects, shapes, faces, smells or sounds.

In my medical practice, I often observe patients with early dementia blame others for their mistakes. Frequently, they have behavior changes like depression or anxiety. In more advanced cases, they cannot find the way home when driving a familiar route (impairment of what is called topographic memory).

THE REAL PANDEMIC IS UNAWARENESS

The treatment for Alzheimer's includes:

Nutrition

Proper nutrition can reduce the risk for Alzheimer's (brain food). Green-leafy vegetables (broccoli, spinach and kale have plenty of vitamin A and C).

Berries are powerful antioxidants and protect the brain.

Nuts contain healthy fats, antioxidants and fibers, which may lower the cholesterol and protect the heart. When we protect the heart, (controlling the blood pressure and cholesterol, keeping the blood vessels healthier), we subsequently end up protecting the brain.

Several studies showed that eating food rich with fibers can reduce brain inflammation and decrease the risk for developing age-related neurodegenerative diseases like Alzheimer's disease.

Whole grain is a great source of fibers. Beans are high in protein, fibers and low in calories and fat. It is important to eat foods with a high content of omega-3 fatty acid.

There are three types of omega-3 fatty acids: ALA (alpha-linolenic acid) mainly found in plants, while DHA (docosahexaenoic acid) and EPA (eicosapentaenoic acid) are mainly found in animal foods.

Omega-3 is found in high concentrations in the brain and all the cell membranes (the lining of the cells). We need a proper function of cells to be healthier. A good concentration of the fatty acids can protect our heart and brain, and can fight cancer and lower the bad cholesterol, keeping the walls of the arteries healthier.

Foods rich in omega-3 fatty acids are flax seeds, chia seeds, walnuts, shellfish (oysters), salmon, tuna, navy beans, avocado, brussels sprouts, olive oil and tofu (just to mention a few).

Some studies show that coconut oil may improve cognitive function. Some countries that consume high levels of coconut oil have a low incidence of Alzheimer cases. This oil is free of cholesterol and trans-fat, improving the HDL (good cholesterol), acting as a natural antibiotic, antioxidant and improving the body's use of insulin.

There are different types of trans-fat acids.

Trans-fat (trans-fatty acids) can be found in natural (meat from cattle or goats and dairy) or artificial (industrial or hydrogenated trans-fats) foods.

Natural trans-fats are believed to be beneficial for our health.

The artificial trans-fats are hazardous for our health and are found in vegetable oils or processed foods. The excess of this type of fat could cause damage to the lining of the blood vessels (called the endothelium), raise the bad cholesterol (LDL), increase the risk for heart disease, is linked to obesity, and causes inflammation which is the cause of many chronic illness including diabetes mellitus, and arthritis. Some studies showed that high levels of trans-fats in the blood can increase the risk for breast cancer.

Based on some clinical studies, the excess of trans-fats increased the risk of dementia.

Artificial trans-fats do not have any health benefits.

Medication

There are medications for Alzheimer's disease that can improve memory boosting levels of cell-to cell interaction or communication.

One of the most commonly prescribed medications causes an increased level of acetylcholine concentration in the brain, improving memory.

Medications are oriented to stabilize or prevent further deterioration of the memory, but also help to decrease agitation or hallucinations in more ad-vanced cases of Alzheimer diseases.

Environment

One of the most important factors to consider for Alzheimer's patients is the environment (especially in the assisted living facilities or nursing homes). Having a positive environment will help them to be in a better mood because they frequently experience anxiety, agitation, depression and disorientation.

When at home, have family and friends visit a person with Alzheimer's to stimulate socialization, promote laughing and memories, and to avoid carpets since they can trip.

It is important to decrease the glare on the floor because they can get confused with colors. Make room for them to navigate easily, and bring a lot of natural light into their living space.

Always encourage them to engage in physical and mental activities (brain cells act like a muscle; the more they are used, the stronger they become).

The Pill on the Wall:®
The Art and
Colors We Love

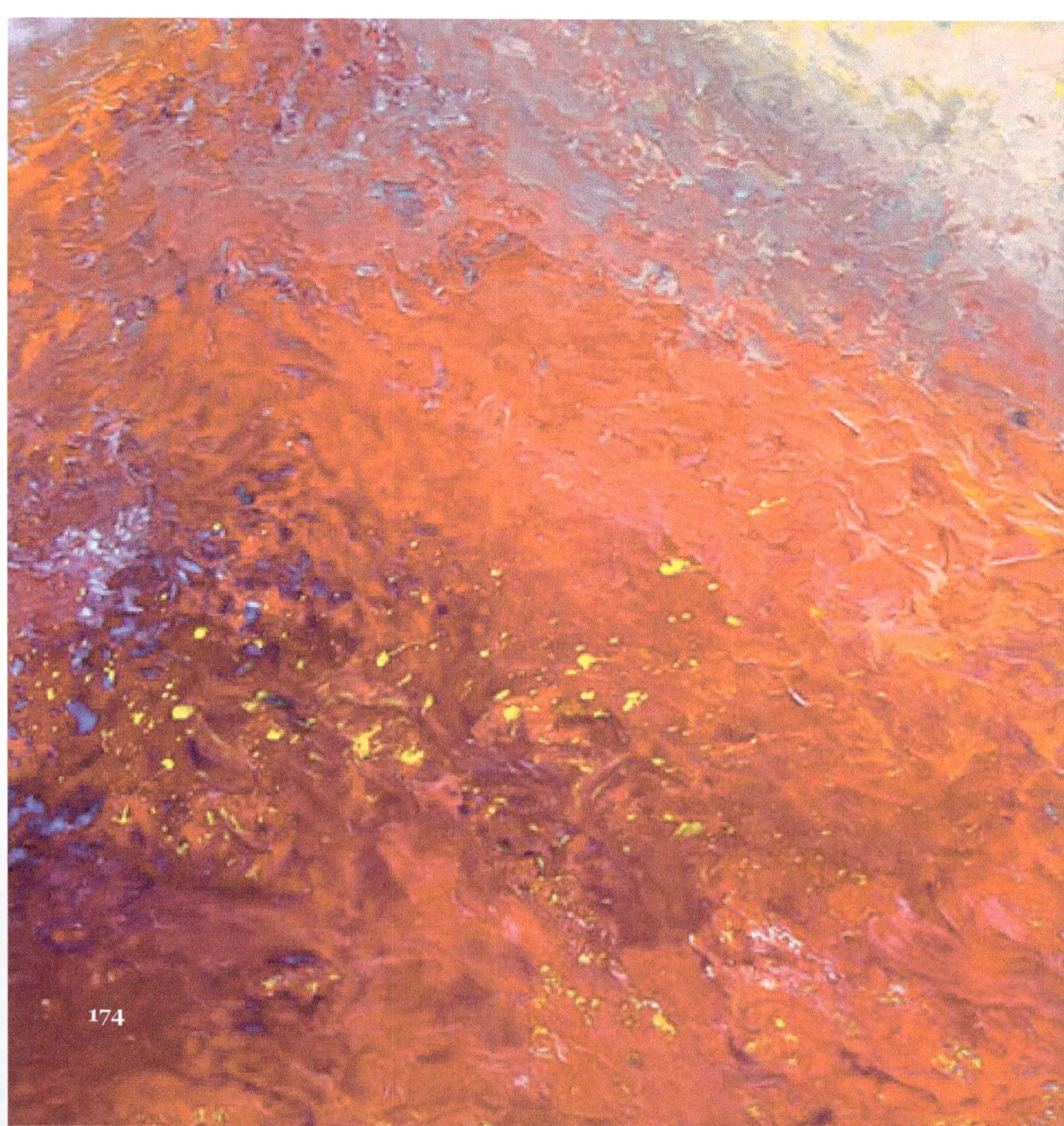

174

The Pill on the Wall®, fueled by Enzology™, is an awareness movement allowing us to think, feel and live better. It explains how the environment plays a crucial role in our health, preventing many illnesses.

As an artist and medical doctor, I was able to merge science, spirituality, quantum physics, nutrition, physiology, psychology, anatomy and medical illnesses into art.

The Pill on the Wall® is my art.

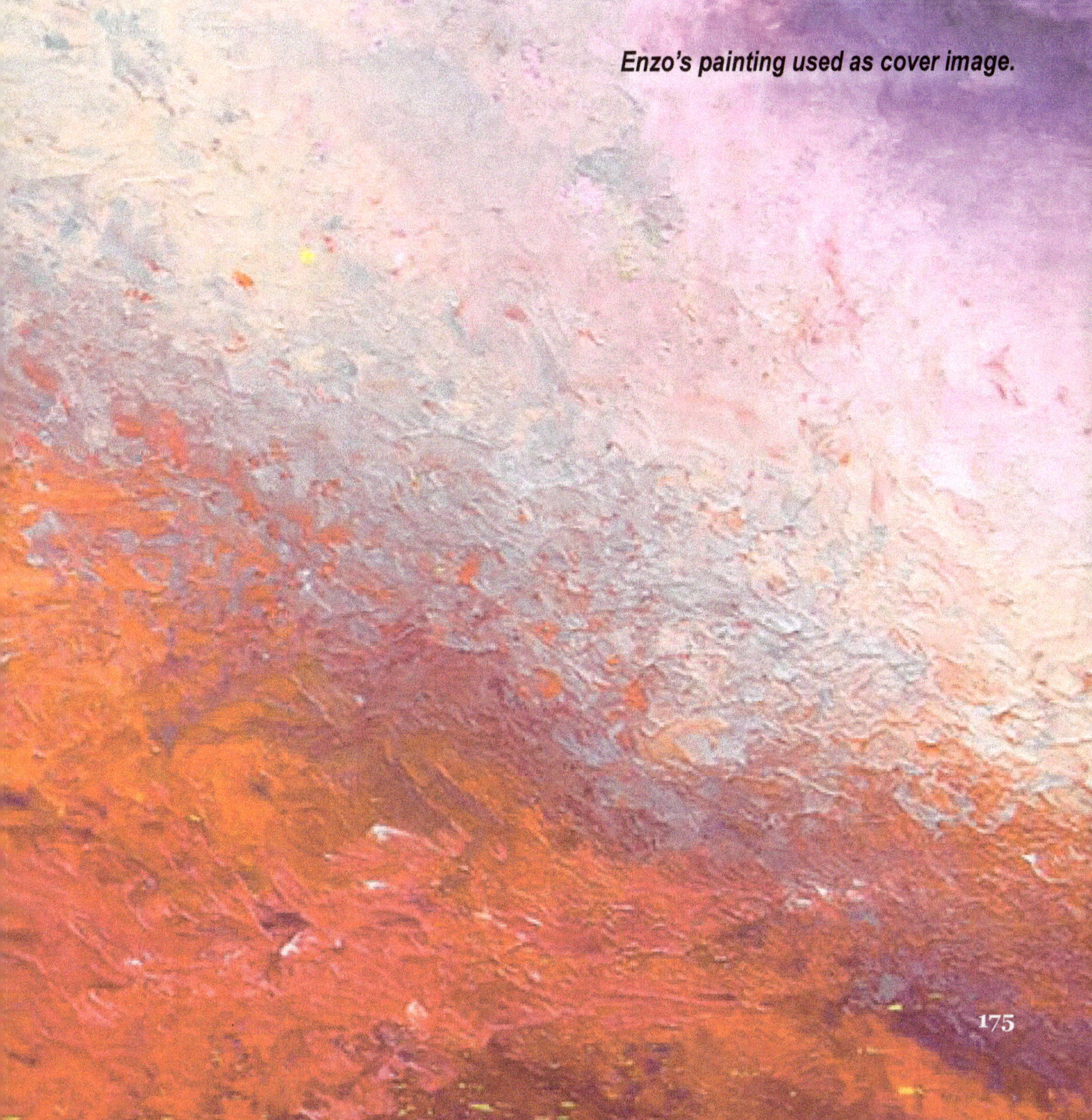

Specifically, the pill is my art and the wall is your environment.

When you become more aware what is around you and how the external environment (your job, home, partner and friends) and your internal environment (your thoughts and emotions) will affect you, then this is when your health and life start to change for the better. You will build your self-esteem, eliminate fear and believe more in yourself.

I believe that faith and awareness will allow you to create harmony in your own energy field – your body.

Following are fifteen images of my paintings that represent my Pill on the Wall® theory.

I have many more paintings, but I chose these images because each one represents a specific meaning or emotion; such as red for excitement, orange for concentration, white for purity, purple for spirituality, blue for relaxation,

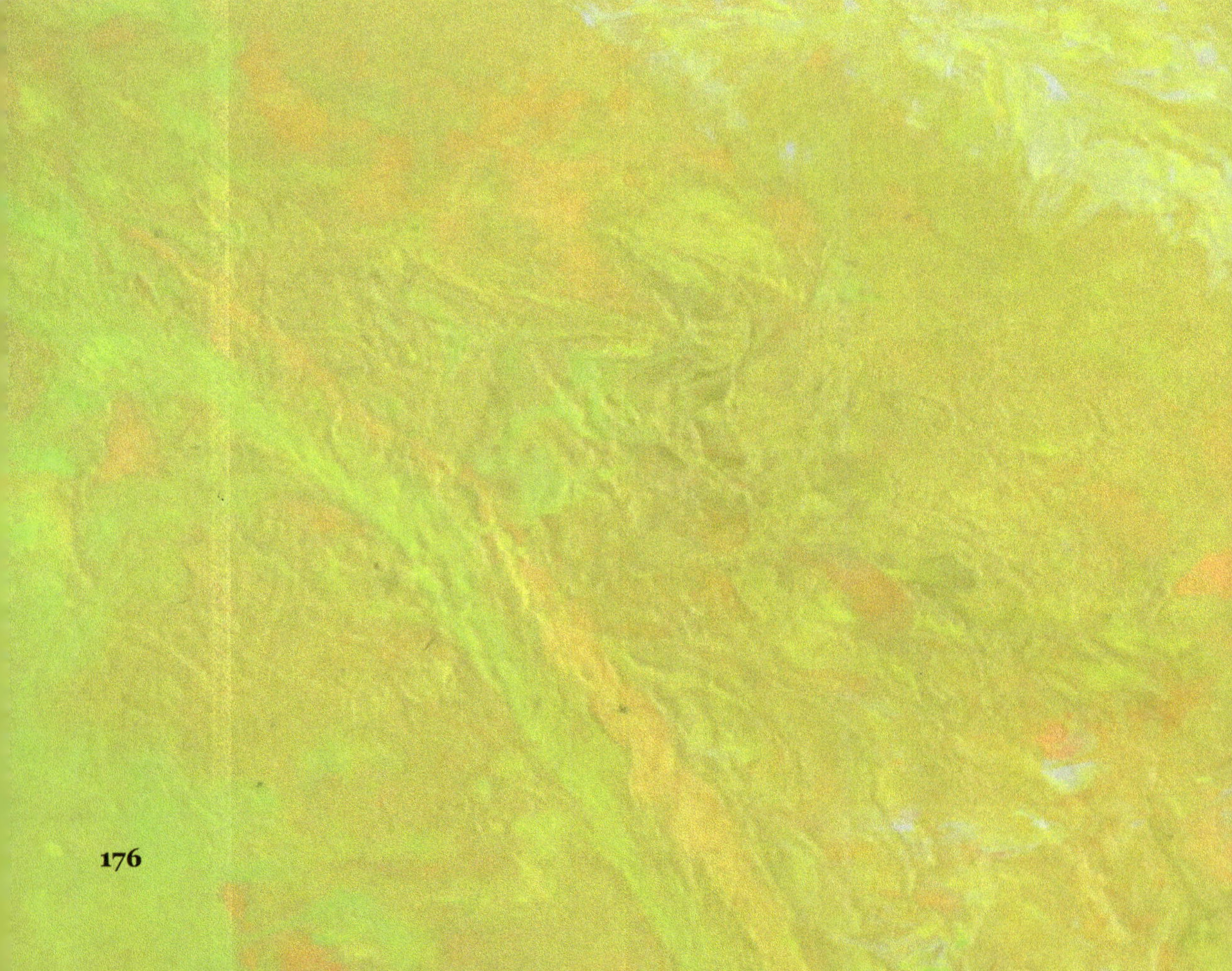

black for prestige or deepness, yellow for happiness , green for peace and wealth and multicolor for action.

I will conclude the chapter with photographs of the house and the restaurant I designed to prove my own theory.

The pictures of the house will show the Pill on the Wall® in use in the kitchen and livingroom. In the restaurant photographs, you will see the friendly enviroment that is enhanced by my Pill on the Wall®.

Both design examples were met with great success. Interaction with patrons, as well as data surveys, showed that people were going to the restaurant for the environment more that for the food.

Likewise, people continued to gather at the house for the atmosphere and environment, which was enhanced by the pleasing decor and friendly socialization.

YELLOW: optimism; fun; energy; happiness; enlightenment

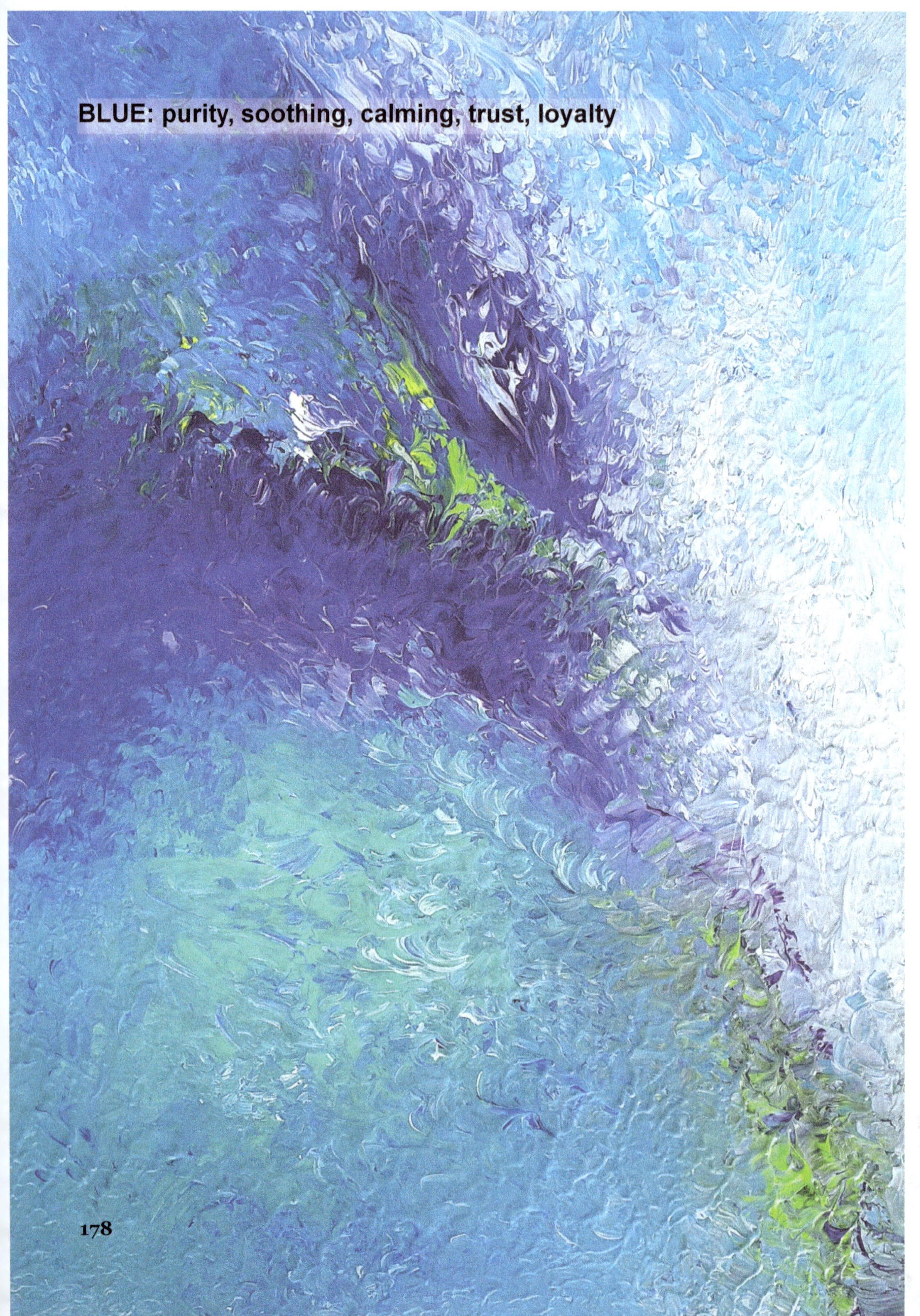
BLUE: purity, soothing, calming, trust, loyalty

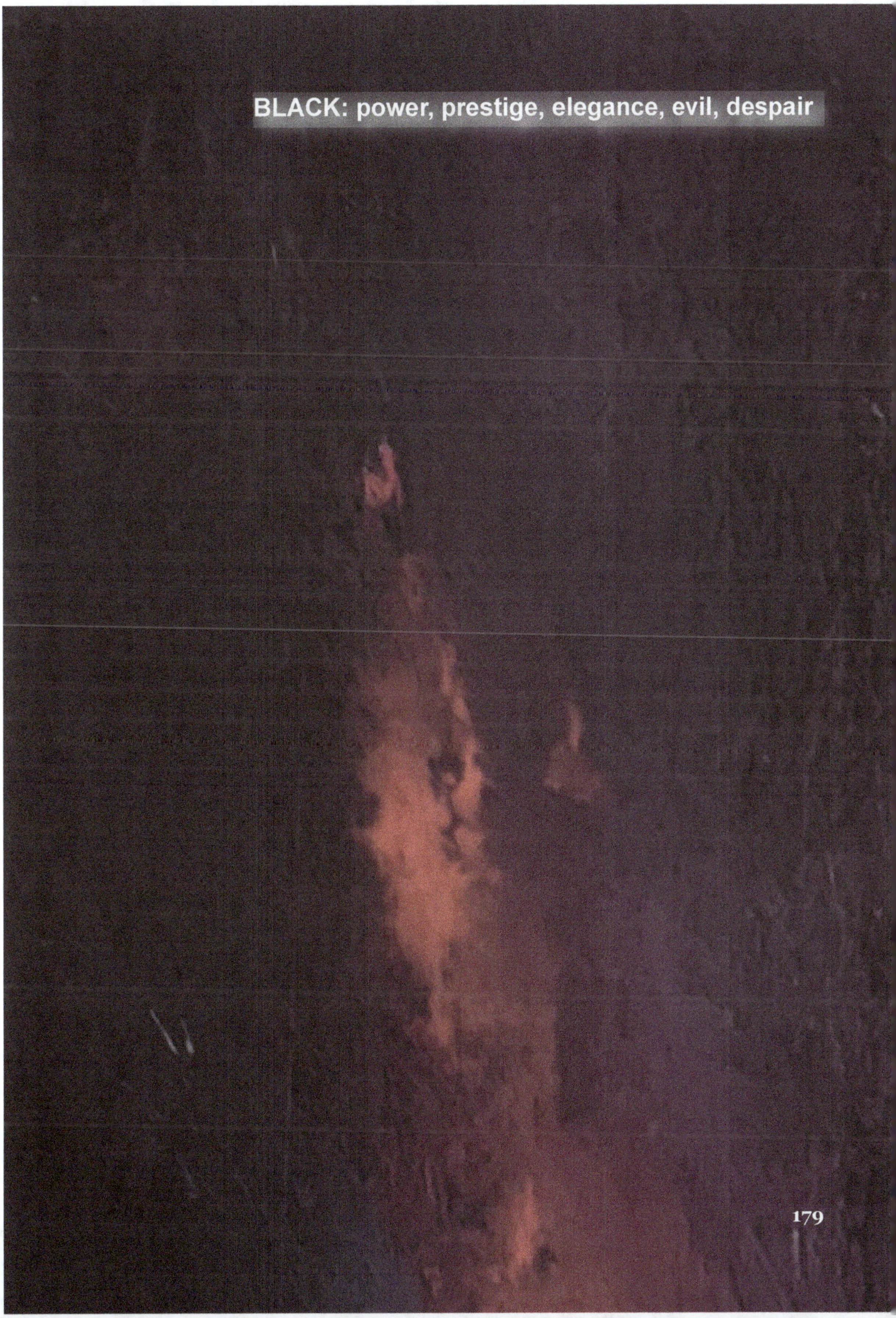

BLACK: power, prestige, elegance, evil, despair

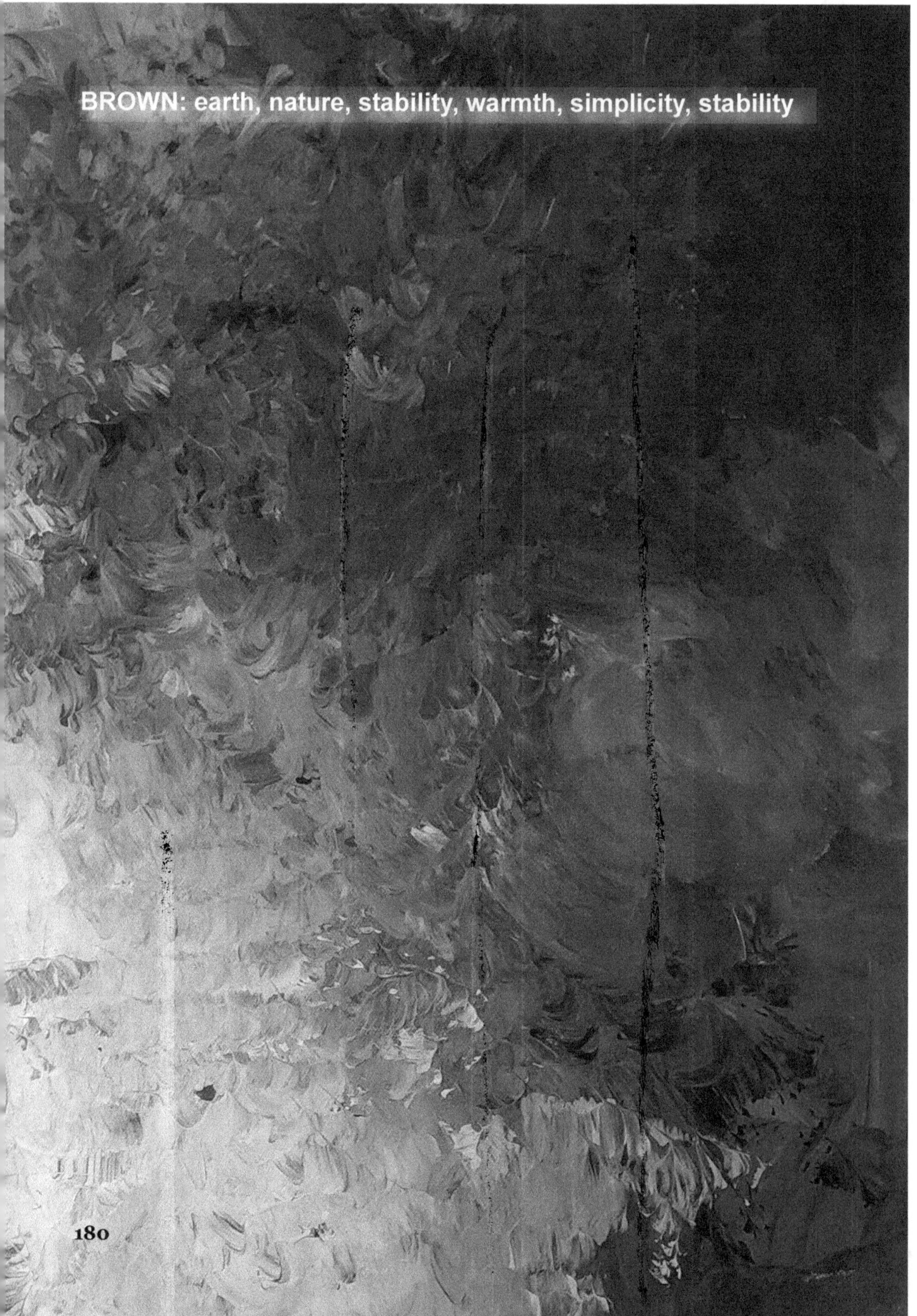
BROWN: earth, nature, stability, warmth, simplicity, stability

GREEN: nature ,harmony, wealth, growth, freshness, calming

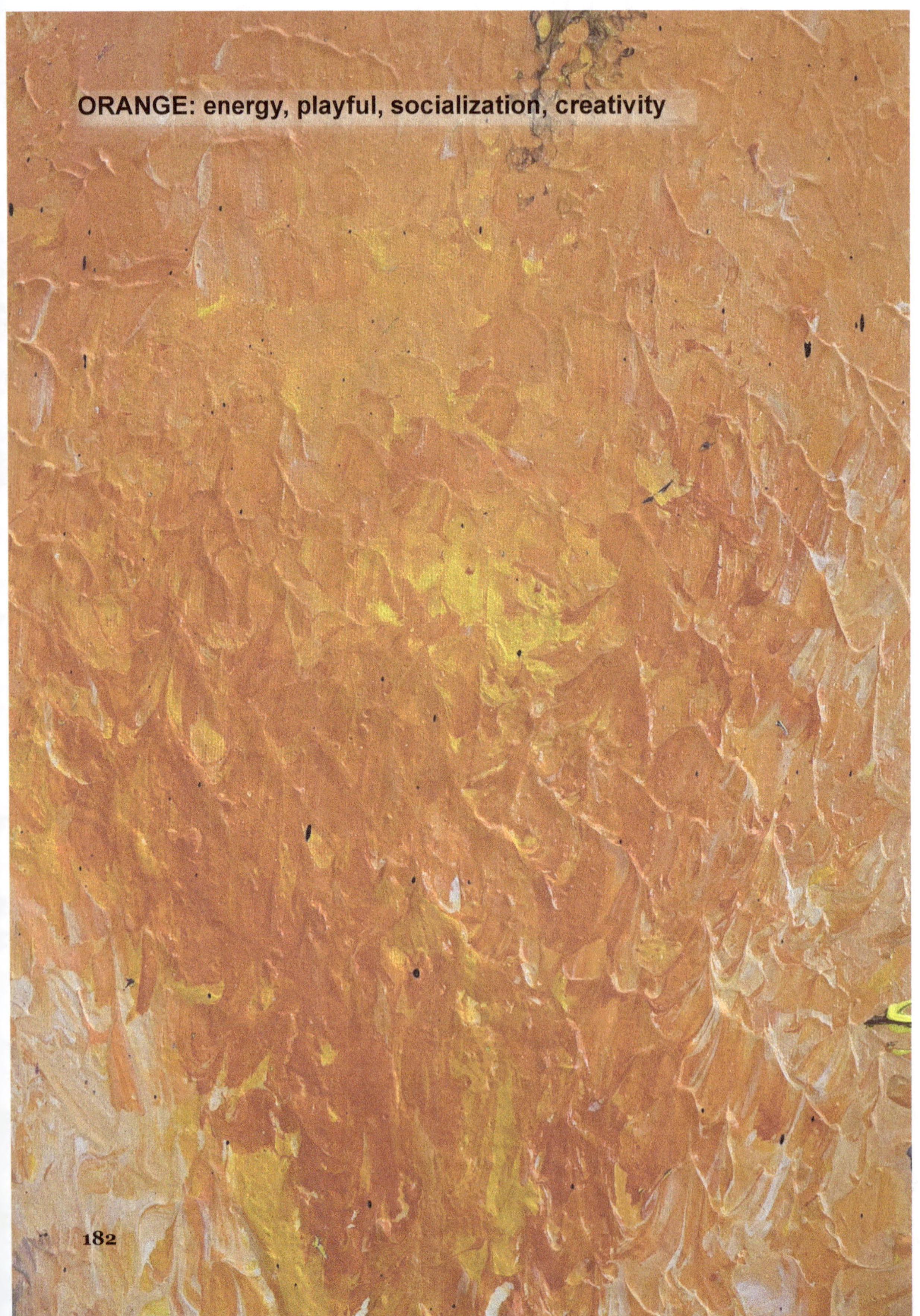
ORANGE: energy, playful, socialization, creativity

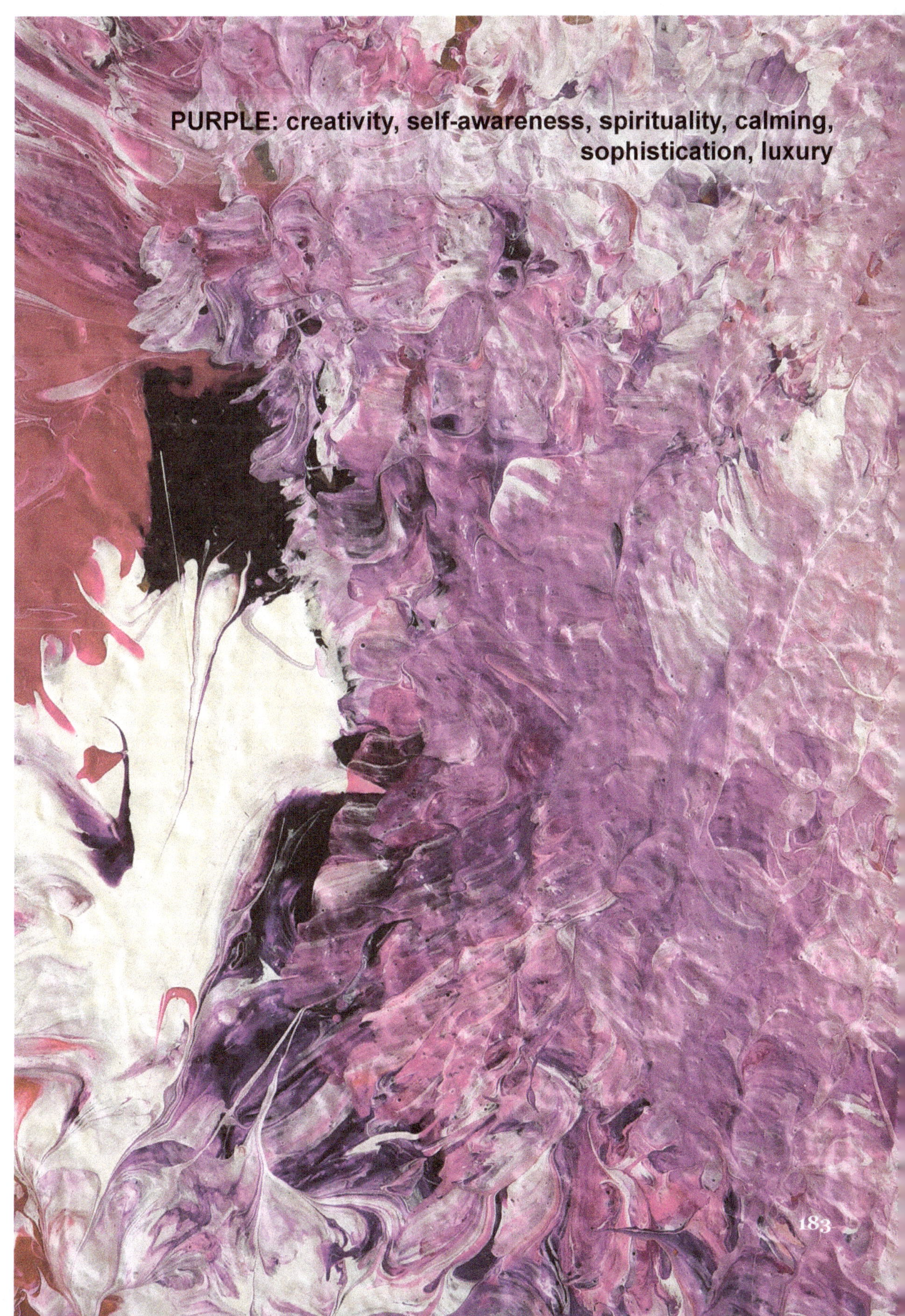
PURPLE: creativity, self-awareness, spirituality, calming, sophistication, luxury

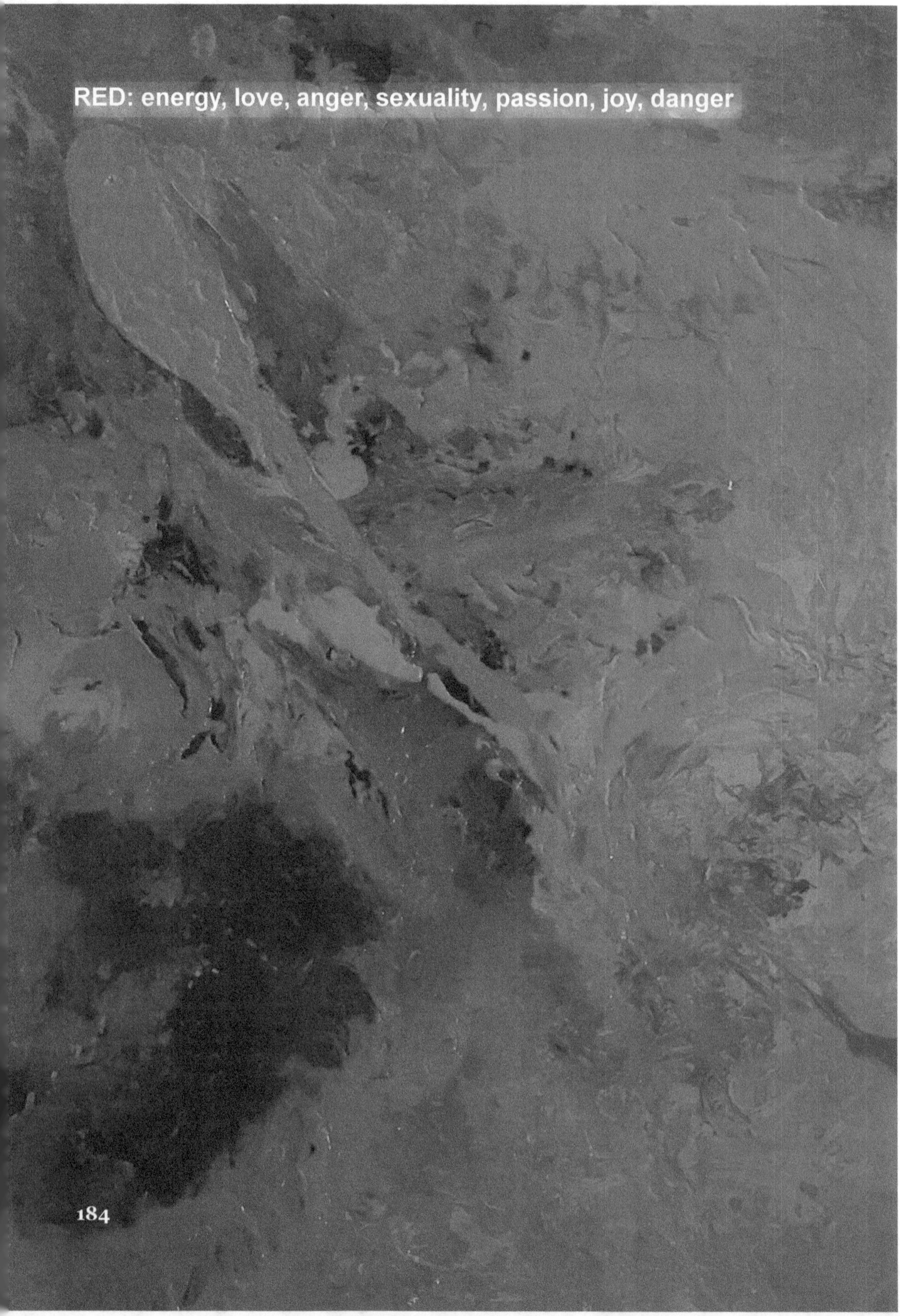

RED: energy, love, anger, sexuality, passion, joy, danger

WHITE: cleanliness, purity, faith, serenity, innocence, goodness, heaven

Because our homes represent our main environment, we should be aware of the colors that surrounded us there.

In the following photographs, I am showing a sample of my Pill on the Wall® (my art) as an awareness of how important the environment is for your health.

It is very important to understand that the environment will change the chemistry in our bodies because it changes the expression of our DNA, which is the body protein factory).

In a previous chapter, I discussed a relative new field called EPIGE-NETICS that explains how the environment can change the expression of our own DNA. I tested that field of study to prove my theory, the Pill on the Wall®.

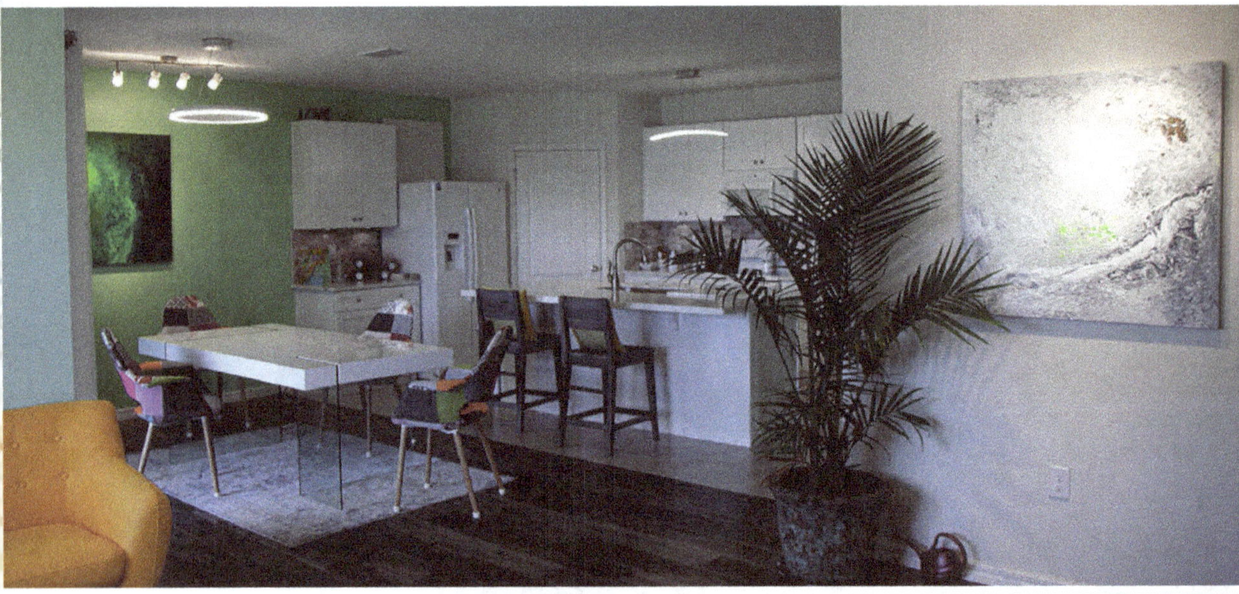

These photographs show the home and its decor and how the paintings enhanced the environment.

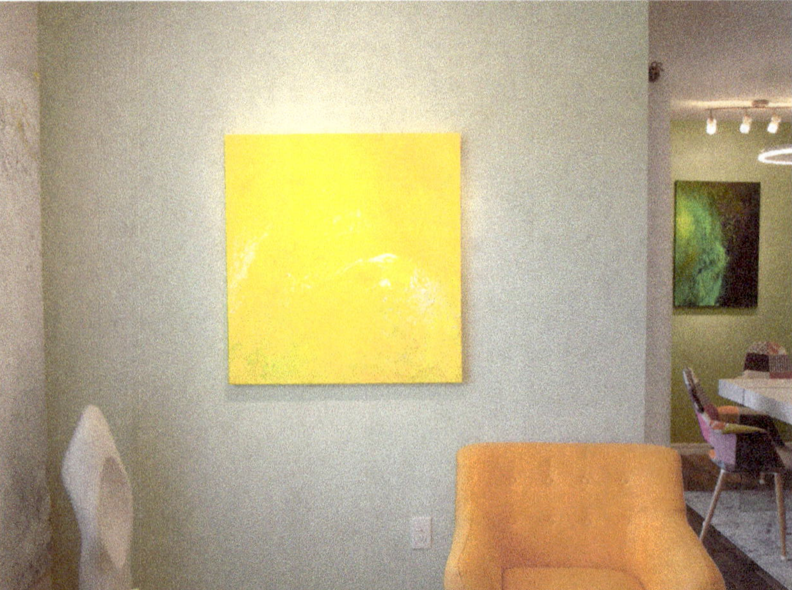

186

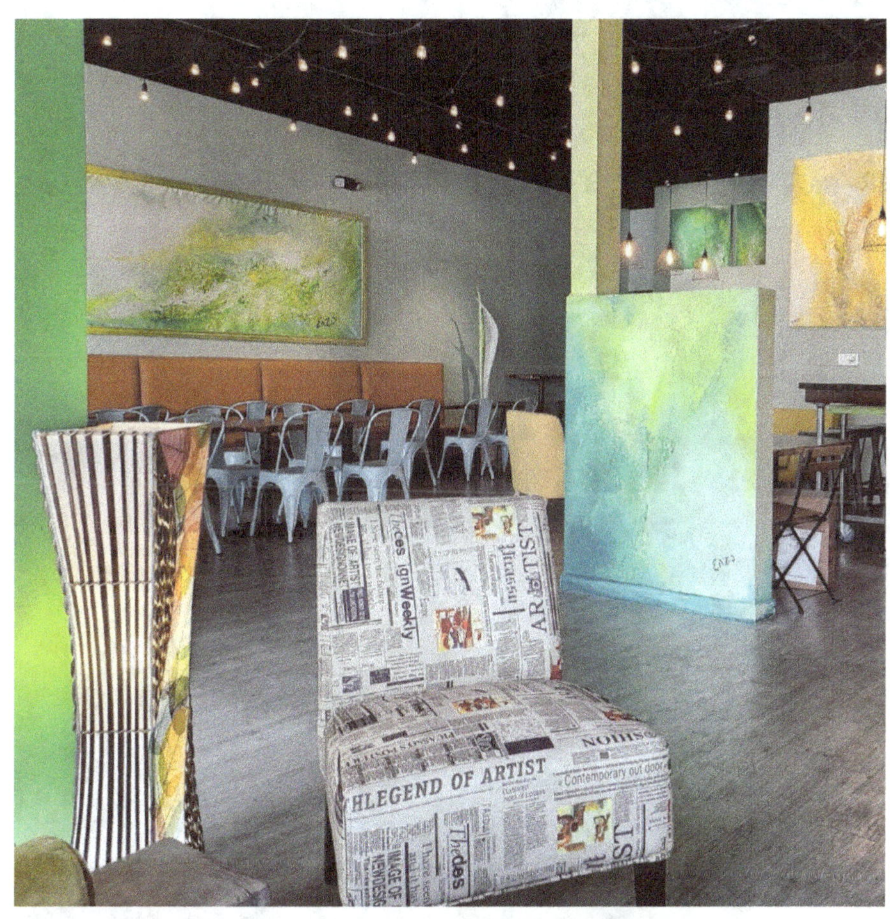

In these photo-graphs, you can see how the Pill on the Wall® sur-rounds restaurant patrons through-out the open space.

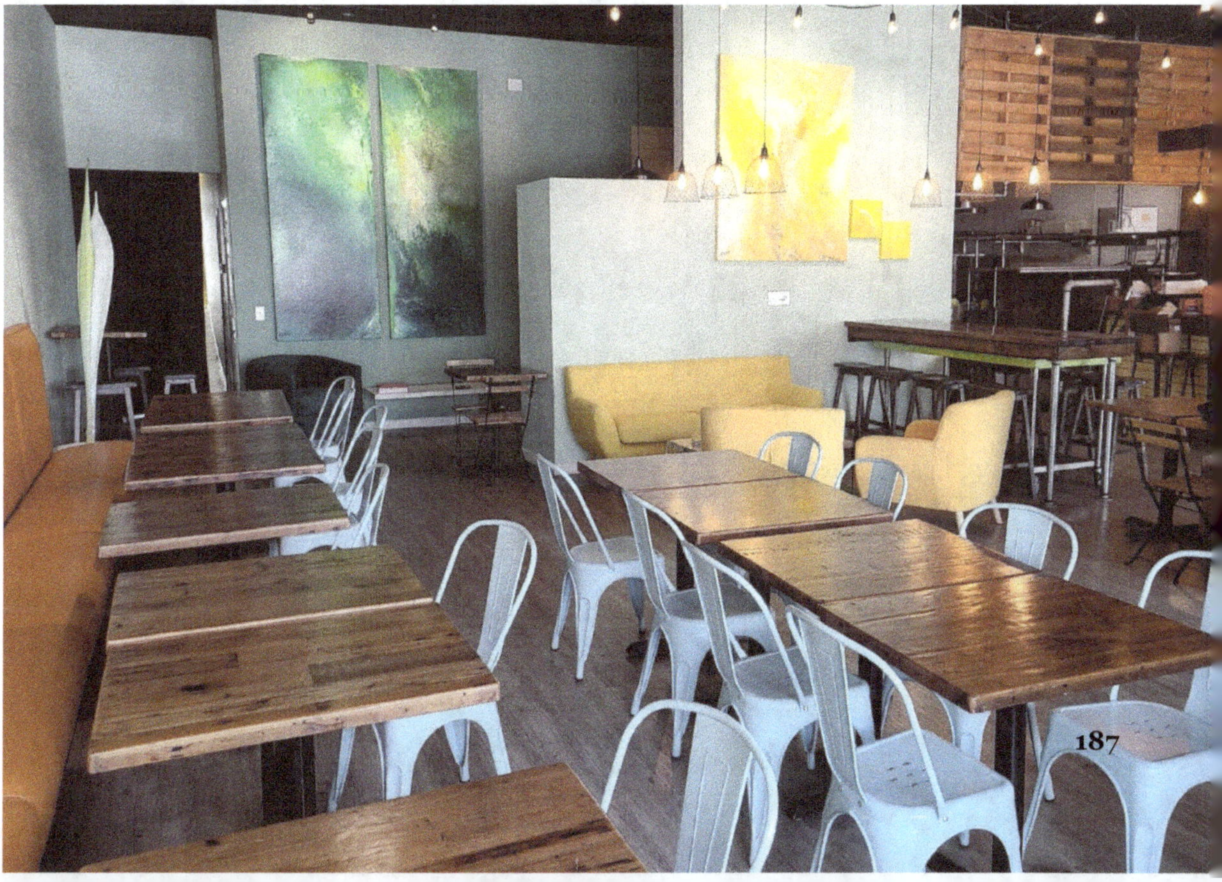

LACK OF LOVE CREATES ILLNESS

References

Tole, E (2004) *The Power of Now: A Guide to Spiritual Enlightenment,* Hodder & Stoughton, 9781444700848

Chopra, D and Tanzi R (2018) *The Healing Self: A Revolutionary New Plan to Supercharge Your Immunity and Stay Well for Life,* Harmony Books, ` 9780451495549

Chopra, D (2015) *The Seven Spiritual Laws of Success: A Pocketbook Guide to Fulfilling Your Dreams,* Amber-Allen Publishing, 9781878424716

Andrews, T (2014) *How to Heal with Color,* Llewellyn Worldwide, 9780738716367

Chopra, D (1989, 2015) *Quantum Healing: Exploring the Frontiers of Mind/Body Medicine,* Bantam Books (1989), Random House (2015), 9781101884973

Dispenza, J (1st edition 2017, 2nd edition 2019) *Becoming Supernatural: How Common People are Doing the Uncommon,* Hay House Inc. 9781401953119

Gimber, T (1994) *Healing with Color and Light: Improve Your Mental, Physical and Spiritual Health,* Fireside, 9780671868574

McTaggart L (2002, 2009) *The Field: The Quest for the Secret Force of the Universe,* HarperCollins, 0061827479, 9780061827471

References, continued ────────────────────────

Baska, P (2011) *The Point of Power: Change Your Thoughts, Change Your Life. Intend, Declare, Detach*, Intelegance Publishing, 9780983247203

Klotsche, C (1994, 2012) *Color Medicine: The Secrets of Color Vibrational Healing*, Metaterra Publications (1994) Light Technology Publishing, LLC (2012), 0929385276, 9780929385273

Bourges, J (1997) *Color Bytes: Blending the Art and Science of Color*, Specialty Marketing Group, 9781888551006

Eckstut, J; Eckstut, A (2013) *The Secret Language of Color: Science, Nature, History, Culture, Beauty of Red, Orange, Yellow, Green, Blue, & Violet*, Black Dog & Leventhal, 9781579129491

Pratt S, Matthews K, (2006) *SuperFoods Rx: Fourteen Foods that Will Change Your Life*, HarperCollins Publishers, 980061172281

Dispenza, J (2012) *Breaking the Habit of Being Yourself: How to Lose Your Mind and Create a New One*, Hay House Inc., 9781401938086

Dispenza, J (2014) *You Are the Placebo: Making Your Mind Matter*, Hay House Inc., 9781401944865

Tolle, E (2003) *Stillness Speaks*, New World Library, 9788188479467, 9781577314004

Dispenza, J (2008) *Evolve Your Brain: The Science of Changing Your Mind,* Health Communications Inc., 9780757307652, 9780757304804

Lipton, B (2016) *Biology of Belief: Unleashing the Power of Consciousness, Matter & Miracles,* Hay House Inc., 9781401952471

Arntz, W., Chasse, B. (Producers), & Arntz W., Chasse B., Vicente M (Directors), 2006, *What the Bleep!? Down the Rabbit Hole,* Samuel Goldwin Company (DVD, Prime Video)

Borek, AJ, et al (2018) *Group-Based Diet and Physical Activity Weight-Loss Interventions: A Systematic Review and Meta-Analysis of Randomised Controlled Trials,* National Library of Medicine, pubmed.ncbi.nlm.nih.gov/29446541

Gudzune, KA, et al (2015) *Efficacy of Commercial Weight-loss Programs: An Updated Systematic Review,* Anals of Internal Medicine, acpjournals.org/doi/10.7326/M14-2238

Lemstra, M, et al (2016) *Weight loss intervention adherence and factors promoting adherence: a meta-analysis,* National Library of Medicine, ncbi.nlm.nih.gov/labs/pmc/articles/PMC4990387

The Well Project (2021) *Starting a Support Group,* a non-profit organization, thewellproject.org/hiv-information/starting-support-group

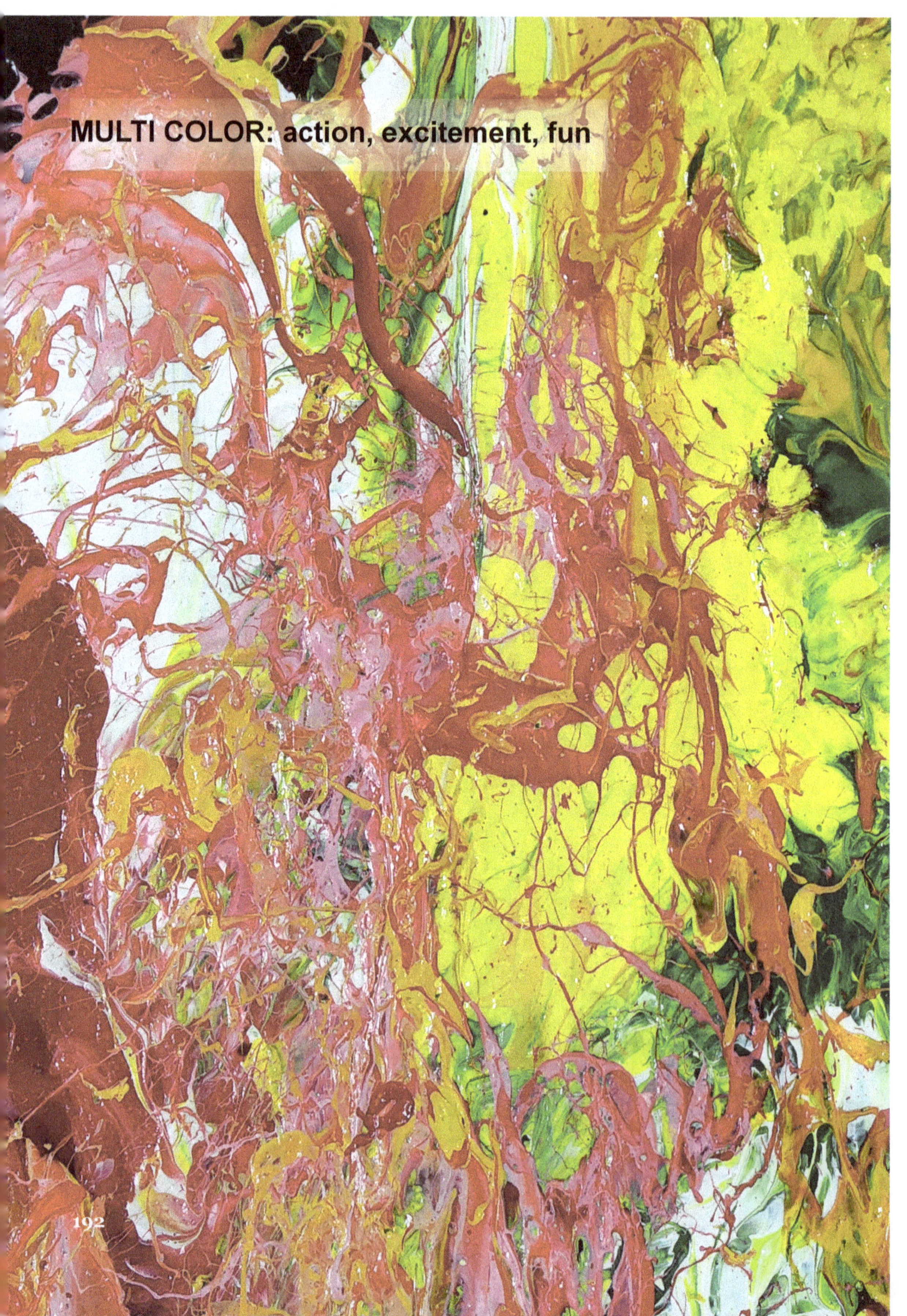
MULTI COLOR: action, excitement, fun

Acknowledgments

The work and books by Drs. Deepak Chopra and Joe Dispenza were a great inspiration to me as I developed my Enzology™ and The Pill on the Wall® theories.

Also, a special acknowledgment to my soul friend, Jacque Dellavalle.

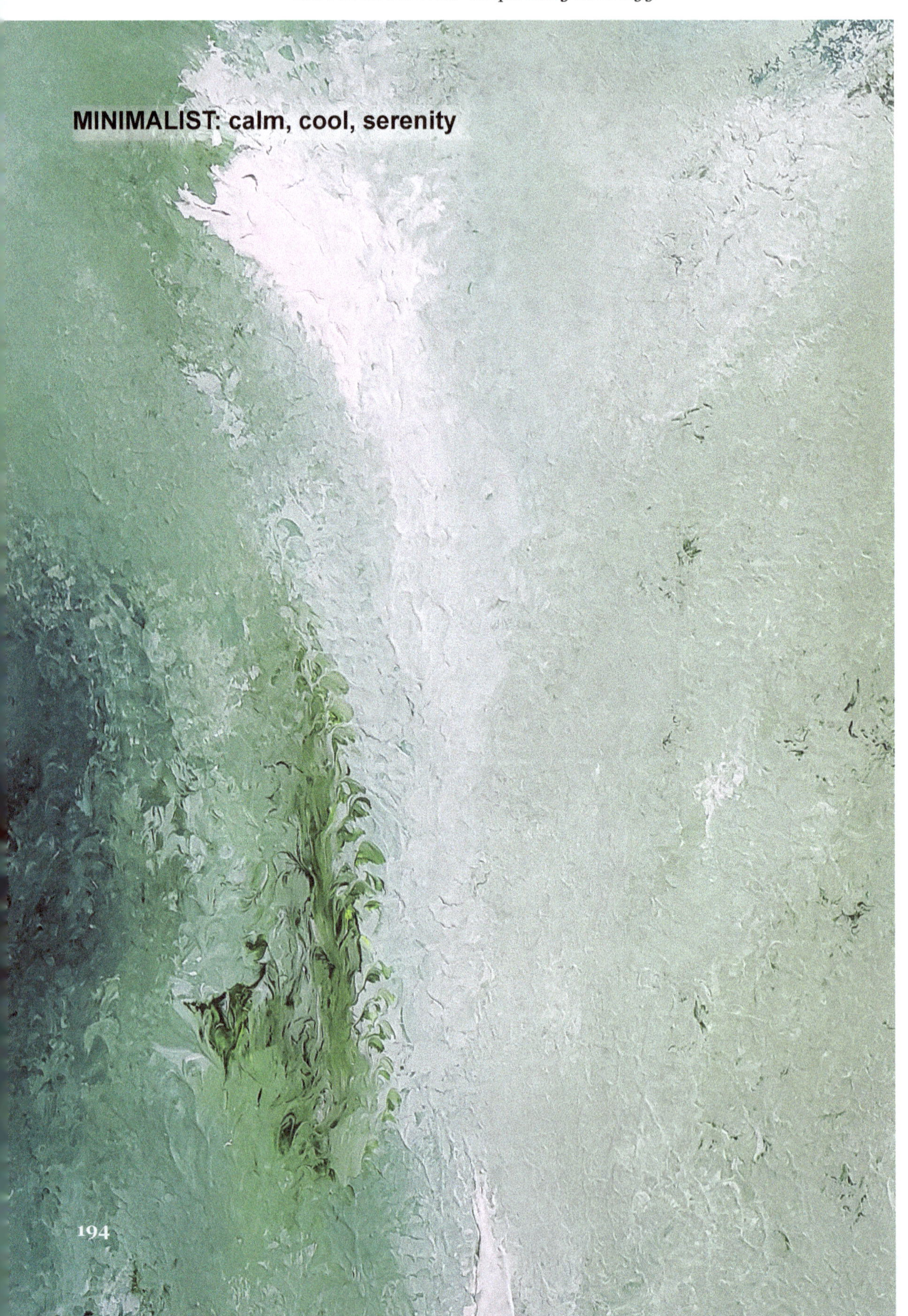
MINIMALIST: calm, cool, serenity

Author's Note

Ever since I can remember I have held artistic potential in my soul. My inspiration comes from my essence – my own being.

As I create a piece, emotions become colors on the canvas. These feelings are displayed as colors without any specific form, as emotion is equally formless.

After I finish shaping a stone or coloring a white canvas, I feel as though I have shared the peace and comfort I feel in my own universe. This potential that I realize, every time I create art, comes from forces inside of me that feel so natural, so automatic, it is like breathing.

Creation to me is liberating, even therapeutic. I feel as though I am taking consciousness, or pure energy, and shaping it into art. This is how I communicate with the world.

I have spent more than ten years writing this book. My main goal is to bring awareness when you are looking at my art (the Pill on the Wall®) and how crucial the environment is for your health through the Enzology™ concept. You can purchase my art through my website: *enzoart.org*.

I hope my art triggers emotions in all who view it. I feel art is a portal to the human soul and I am merely the avenue between the two.

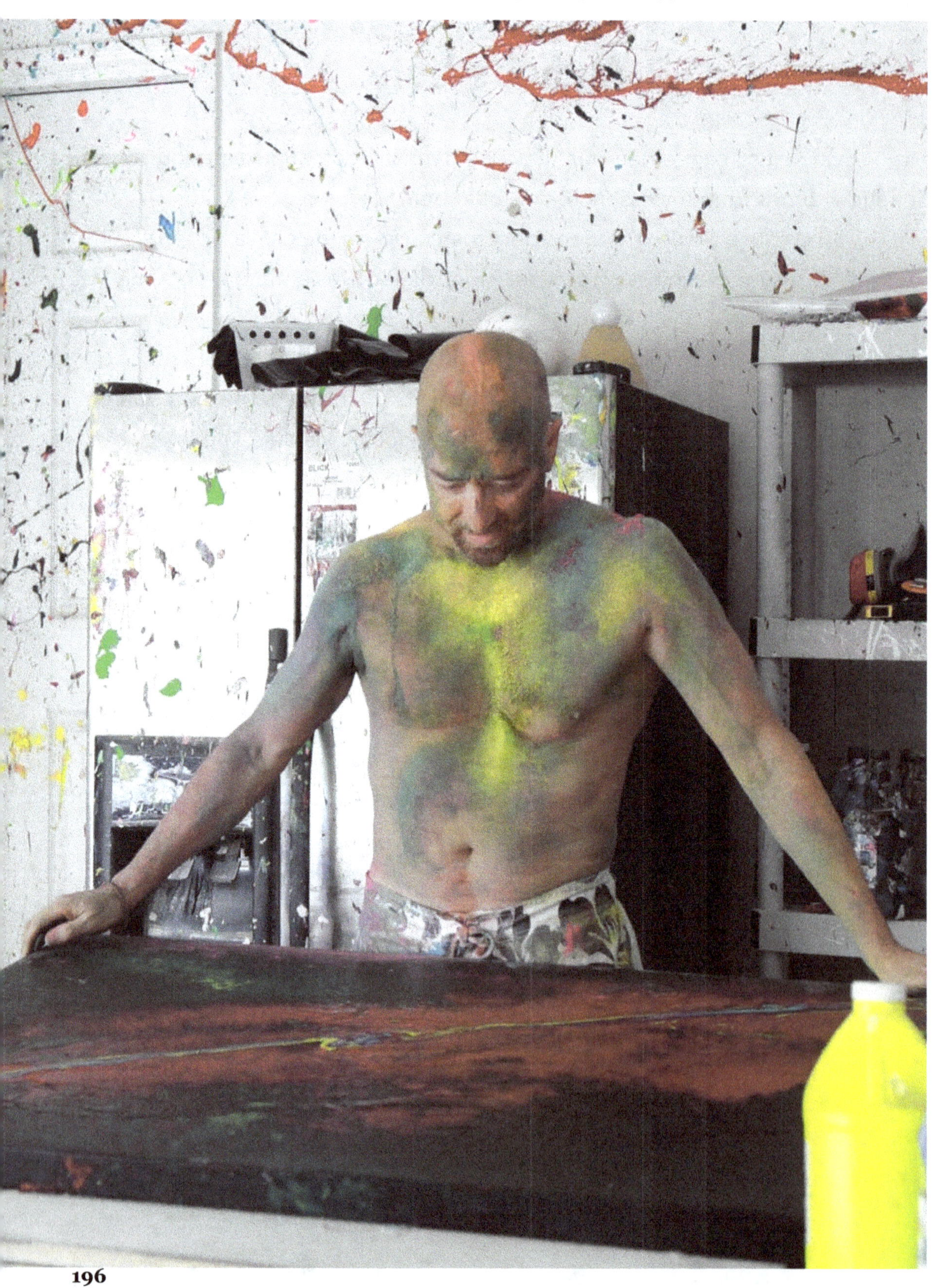

About the Author

Enzo has exhibited his art throughout the world – from his native country of Argentina to Italy, France, Tokyo and Switzerland. In the United States he has exhibited in art galleries and festivals from New York City to Miami and Orlando, Florida. Currently, his art is represented by Studio Abba in Florence, Italy.

He lives and tends to his neurology practice in New Smyrna Beach, a seaside Florida town in Southeast Volusia County, which is known as one of the best art towns in America.

Enzo has been part of his local art community since 2007, exhibiting at IMAGES: A Festival of the Arts, which is one of the longest-continuous running art festival in the state of Florida. He also has exhibited at other Florida art festivals, including local art galleries – The Hub on Canal, in New Smyrna Beach and The Peabody Auditorium in Daytona Beach.

He has a YouTube channel with videos from previous conferences and shows where he explains his theory. His March 2022 conference presentation was at the Museum of Arts & Science in Daytona Beach, Florida. The YouTube video is titled, "Enzology, presentation at the Daytona Museum of Arts and Sciences." His October 2017 YouTube video of his solo art show at Studio Abba in Florence, Italy, is titled "Enzo Trapani in Florence."

Beginning in 2012, Enzo committed to donating five percent of all of his art sales to Corazon de Vida, a US-based nonprofit organization that helps abandoned and orphaned children in Baja, Mexico. Corazon de Vida provides children in dire need the necessities of shelter, food, clothing, education and healthcare – as well as hope. CDV not only financially supports orphanages in Baja, but also provides assistance through frequent cross-border visits by board members, staff and volunteers.

YOU
ARE IN
THE
NOW